Conversations On Botany

CONVERSATIONS

ON

BOTANY.

Printed by A. Strahan,
New-Street-Square, London.

CONVERSATIONS

ON

BOTANY.

WITH PLATES.

SECOND EDITION.

LONDON:
PRINTED FOR LONGMAN, HURST, REES, ORME, AND BROWN,
PATERNOSTER-ROW.
1818.

ADVERTISEMENT.

A SECOND EDITION of this volume has been called for so much sooner than the Authors had reason to expect, that some of the suggestions for its improvement, which they had solicited from their friends, did not arrive until the greater part of this impression was printed: — But, they have endeavoured to correct some of the principal errors; and, if another edition be required, they hope to render their work more deserving of approbation.

30th May, 1818.

THE object of the following pages, is to enable children and young persons to acquire a knowledge of the vegetable productions of their native country, by introducing to them, in a familiar manner, the principles of the Linnæan System of Botany.

For this purpose, the arrangement of Linnæus is briefly explained; a native plant of each class (with a few exceptions) is examined, and illustrated by an Engraving; and a short account is added, of some of the principal foreign species.

It is not without regret, that the classification of Linnæus has been in part relinquished, in order to conform to that adopted by Dr. Withering; who has distributed the plants of four of the Linnæan classes, Gynandria, Monoecia, Dioecia, and Polygamia, among the preceding classes, according to the number of their stamens: his valuable "Arrangement of British Plants" being at present one of the best works of reference upon this subject, for persons unacquainted with Latin. But, it is to be hoped, that Sir James Edward Smith will soon furnish to the English reader*, a systematical account of all our native plants, according to the original method of Linnæus.

What Miss Edgeworth has said of Chemistry, may with equal truth be applied to Botany, and may serve to recommend the study of it, as a branch of general education: — "It is not a science of parade, it affords occupation and infinite variety, it demands no bodily strength, it can be pursued in retirement; — there is no danger of its inflaming the imagination, because

* See "Introduction, &c. to Botany," 3d edition, Preface, page xi.

the mind is intent upon realities. The knowledge that is acquired is exact; and the pleasure of the pursuit is a sufficient reward for the labour." *

1*st March*, 1817.

It may be due to the author of the admirable "Conversations on Chemistry," to mention, that the title of the present volume was chosen, because it was the only one that seemed to be adapted to the nature of the subject, which had not been appropriated by preceding writers.

* "Letters for Literary Ladies," 3d edit. page 60.

ERRATA.

Page 2. last line. for "wheh," read "when."
21. line 12. for "same," read "first."
30. line 13. for "composed," read "formed."
77. last line but one, for "Eulgaris," read "vulgaris."
79. The *number* of this page is omitted.
80. line 6. for "Maple-tree," read "Maple."
101. Insert an asterisk of reference (*) before the note.
105. line 4 from bottom, after the word "tearing," insert a semicolon.
208. line 3 from bottom, for "f" read "of."

CONTENTS.

LIST OF THE PLATES.

The two parts of Plate 2. are to face each other.

EXPLANATION

OF THE

TABLE OF THE CLASSES. — PLATE 2.

This Plate represents the flower of a native plant, in each of the twenty-four classes, viz.

Class 1. A Flower of the Hippu'ris vulga'ris — *Common Mare's-tail*, slightly magnified.
2. ——— Veroni'ca officina'lis — *Common Speedwell*, magnified.
3. ——— Valeria'na officina'lis — *Great wild Valerian*, magnified.
4. ——— Cornus sanguin'ea — *Wild Cornel-tree.*
5. ——— Polemo'nium cærul'eum — *Jacob's-ladder.*
6. ——— Scilla bifo'lia — *Two-leaved Squill.*
7. ——— Trienta'lis Europæ'a — *Chickweed Winter-green.*
8. ——— Chlora perfolia'ta — *Yellow Centaury.*
9. ——— Bu'tomus umbella'tus — *Flowering Rush.*

Class 10. A Flower of the Saxif'raga stella'ris — *Hairy Saxifrage.*

11. ———— Sempervi'vum Tecto'rum —*Common House-leek.*

12. ———— Pru'nus insiti'tia — *Bullace Plum.*

13. ———— Chelido'nium ma'jus — *Common Celandine.*

14. ———— Teu'crium scorodo'nia — *Wood Sage.*

15. ———— Cardam'ine praten'sis — *Common Cardamine.*

16. ———— Althæ'a officina'lis — *Marsh-Mallow.*

17. ———— Genis'ta tincto'ria—*Dyer's Greenweed.*

18. ———— Hyper'icum pulchrum — *Upright St. John's wort.*

19. ———— Sonchus cæru'leus — *Blue Sow-Thistle.*

20. ———— Orchis mas'cula — *Early Purple-Orchis.*

21. A spike of Flowers of the Ca'rex pulica'ris, *Flea-Seg*;—with two flowers magnified; one having stamens only, the other only a pistil.

22. Two Catkins, from different plants, of the Sa'lix argen'tea, *Silky Sand-Willow*; one bearing flowers with stamens, the other with pistils; with a single flower of each kind magnified.

23. A Spike of Flowers, of the At'riplex pat'ula, *Halberd-leaved Orache*; with two flowers, of different kinds, magnified.

In this genus, (which is the only native one of the class Polygamia,) none of the flowers have stamens only.

Class 24. A small specimen of a Fern, Asple'nium tri choma'nes, *Common Maiden-hair;* and of a Moss, Hy'pnum bryö'i'des, *Dwarf Hypnum;* both of the natural size.

PRONUNCIATION
OF THE
LATIN NAMES OF PLANTS.

It will be necessary for persons unacquainted with the Latin language, to observe the following rules, in pronouncing the botanical names of plants:—

1. The letter *e*, at the end of a word, is always to be sounded; for example, the word *Ga'le* is to be pronounced as if composed of two syllables, *Ga'-le*; and not like the English word *Gale*.

2. When the letters *c* and *h* come together, they are to be pronounced hard, like *k*. Thus, Li'chen, is pronounced Li'ken.

3. When the vowels *a* and *e*, *o* and *e*, or *e* and *i*, occur together, if not marked with two dots placed over them, (as in *Daböe'cia* pronounced *Da-bo-e'-cia*,) they are so be pronounced as one sound. Thus

Cratae'gus, is to be pronounced Cra-te'-gus.
Monoe'cia - - - Mo-ne'-cia.
Cheiran'thus - - - Ki-ran'-thus;—
with the *i* long, like the word *Eye*.

4. In words that end in *-ides*, the *i* is always to be pronounced long, like the word Eye;—eye-des; thus *Lichenöi'des*, is to be pronounced *Liken-o-Eye-des*.

In this volume, wherever the accentuation of the Latin names or terms is not obvious, they are divided and marked, as they are to be pronounced; and the accent or force of the voice, is to be thrown upon that syllable or letter which precedes the mark:—Thus

Ar'butus, is to be pronounced *Ar'*butus, not Ar*bu'*tus.
Veroni'ca - - - Ver*oni'*ca, not Ver*on'*ica.

CONVERSATIONS

ON

BOTANY.

CONVERSATION THE FIRST.

BOTANY IN GENERAL. — LINNÆUS. — USES OF BOTANY. — PARTS OF A FLOWER.

EDWARD.

WHAT are you doing, mamma?

MOTHER.

I am examining the pretty little yellow flower, that we found this morning in the hedge.

EDWARD.

How do you examine a flower?

MOTHER.

You cannot understand the method, my dear, until you have learned something of Botany.

EDWARD.

What is Botany?

MOTHER.

It is the science that makes us acquainted with plants, and teaches us how to distinguish them from one another. The term Botany is derived from a Greek word signifying an herb or grass. Do you not recollect what your aunt and I were talking of yesterday in the garden? I thought you seemed attentive to our conversation.

EDWARD.

You said something about a very industrious man, who had examined a great many plants.

MOTHER.

Yes: — we were speaking of Linnæus, a celebrated botanist, who did so much to increase our knowledge of the works of nature, that he was called the *Father of Natural History*. He was born in Sweden, in the year 1707.

EDWARD.

Am I too young to learn botany? I think I should like it very much.

MOTHER.

By no means, my dear. It is so simple a study, that the youngest persons can understand it, whe the principles are properly explained to them; and if you like, I will teach you all I know of it. Linnæus himself was scarcely four years old, when he heard his father describing to a friend some flowers, which he had just gathered from the turf where they sat. This first botanical lecture made such an impression upon him, that afterwards, he used to ask his father the names and properties of all the plants he could procure: and even at that early age, he began to attend to the habits and distinctions of animals and insects also.

EDWARD.

What is the use of botany?

MOTHER.

You are not yet old enough to understand all its uses, but I will endeavour to tell you some of them. You will be surprised to learn the variety of purposes to which plants are applied; they form the principal part of our food, medicine, cloathing, and furniture, and several of the most beautiful dyes are obtained from them: but in some instances, the different kinds resemble each other so nearly, that ignorant persons have often mistaken those which are hurtful or of no value, for the useful ones. Some animals are guided by an instinct that teaches them what to choose, and what to avoid; but men must have recourse for this purpose, to their own experience or the observations of others; and without a knowledge of botany, we could neither understand the descriptions given by other persons, nor describe them ourselves so as to be understood. As an amusement, Botany has many recommendations: it may be studied with less expense than most other sciences; it invites us into the country, and increases the pleasure of every walk; and the cultivation of plants in the garden affords one of the most innocent and healthful occupations that we can enjoy.—Indeed, the study of natural history in general is so attractive, that those who once engage in it seldom give it up. The sameness of most other pursuits becomes at last fatiguing; but the naturalist meets with endless variety, and at every step he discovers beautiful contrivances in the works of nature, that escape the attention of common observers.

EDWARD.

But when do you think I shall be able to examine a plant as you do now, mamma? Is it very difficult?

MOTHER.

At first it may appear so to you; but do not be frightened at the undertaking; you will soon find that it is not a great one. Nothing is required but to have patience;—to begin at the beginning:

after that you need not go any farther than you choose. An indolent person, it is true, can never expect to become a good botanist, nor, indeed, to be good for any thing. When Linnæus was about to publish one of his most celebrated works *, he examined the characters of eight thousand flowers: so that you may judge how very industrious he must have been. If you are attentive, and try to remember what I shall tell you, I think that at the end of a month you may be able to examine the flowers that you meet with in your walks, without my assistance.

EDWARD.

I long to begin! Will you take a walk with me to-morrow in the fields, to bring home some flowers?

MOTHER.

With pleasure, my dear; I am very glad to see you so eager to begin this delightful study: but before we set out, you had better learn the names of the different parts of a plant. You already know, that the root is that part which grows in the ground, and supplies the rest with nourishment. The stem rises from the root, and is generally clothed with green leaves. The flower is the beautifully coloured part that you so often admire: it is divided into several different parts, which I will explain to you, if you will go into the garden, and bring me a branch of any plant you like.

* *Genera Plantarum* (Genera of Plants).

EDWARD.

Here, mamma, is some Wall-flower; it is the first that I could find in blow.

MOTHER.

It will do very well; but if we had a larger flower you could see the different parts more distinctly. [See PLATE 1.] You may now break off one of the flowers, and hold it by the little stalk, between your thumb and finger. The green part, that you see close under the yellow blossom, and which is not unlike a cup, is called the Calyx. The yellow leaves that grow out of it, are called Petals or blossom-leaves; the petals altogether form what is called the Corolla or Blossom. Pull off very gently from the little stalk, the calyx and petals, and you will see seven threads; one in the middle thicker than the rest, and the other six with yellow heads: those with heads are called Stamens, and are each composed of two parts, the heads called Anthers, and the threads which support them Filaments: as this pen-knife is divided into two parts, the handle and the blade, which are together called a knife. The centre thread is called the Pistil, and consists of three parts; the Germen or seed-bud, which is the thickest green part at the bottom, the Style which stands upon it, and the Summit, or top of the style. When the petals fall off, after the plant has been in flower

PLATE 1

Parts of a Flower.

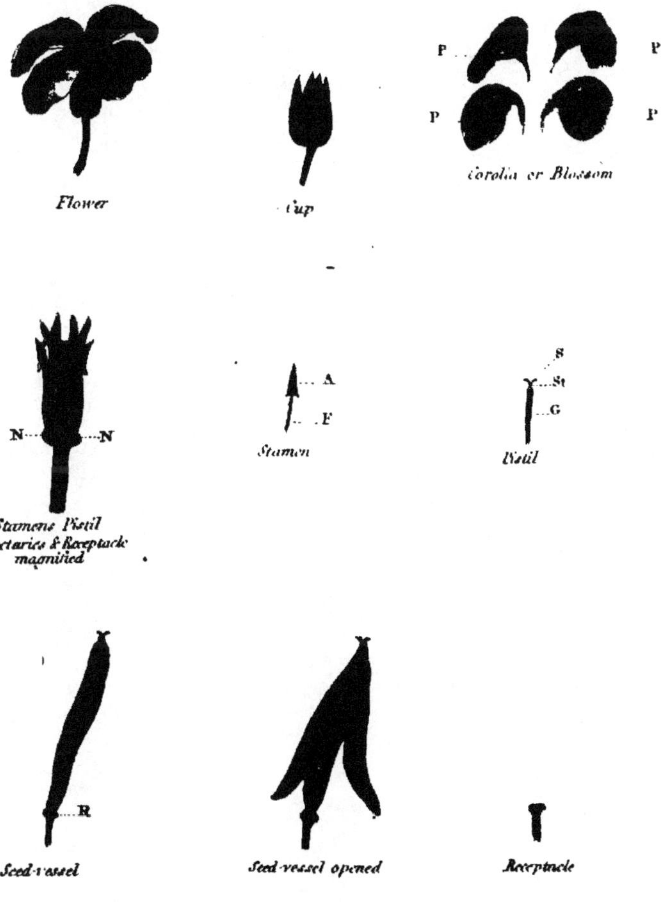

The Flower here shown is that of the Common Wall Flower.

for some time, the germen grows larger, and is then called the Seed-vessel, because it contains the seeds within it. In the wall-flower, the seed-vessel is a long pod, containing several flat seeds. If you now pull off the stamens and pistil, you may perceive what is named the Receptacle; it is that part at the top of the stalk, to which all the rest of the flower is fixed.

EDWARD.

I have done so; — but I do not see any thing remarkable.

MOTHER.

You are right. In many flowers the receptacle is not very conspicuous, and the wall-flower is one of them; but in others it is very large, particularly in the Artichoke, which you sometimes see at dinner. What we commonly call the bottom, that is, the part which remains after we have taken off the leaves and bristly substance or choke, is the receptacle.

There is also another part, which, as well as the receptacle, is indistinct in the wall-flower. It is called the Nectary, and its use is supposed to be to prepare a sweet fluid like honey or nectar, which it frequently contains. It is from this part that bees collect their honey. The form of the nectary varies in different flowers; in some it is very conspicuous, in others less visible, and in many it appears to be entirely wanting. The nectaries of the wall-flower are two little greenish bodies surrounding the lower part of the short stamens; but as you cannot easily see them, I shall take an opportunity, when we examine a plant that has larger nectaries, of pointing them out to you. There are many flowers whose parts are so small, that they cannot be seen distinctly without the help of a magnifying glass: here is one that you shall have to assist you; and you will find a needle and a sharp-pointed pen-knife also very useful; for some flowers are too delicate to be divided by the fingers alone.

CONVERSATION THE SECOND.

LINNÆAN ARRANGEMENT OF PLANTS.—CLASSES.—ALTERATIONS ADOPTED BY DR. WITHERING.—ORDERS.—GENERA.—SPECIES.

EDWARD.

WHEN I have examined a plant, mamma, how am I to find out its name?

MOTHER.

Before you can do so, you must learn how the vegetables that are known have been arranged; and I will now explain to you as clearly as I can, the system of Linnæus, which is the one almost universally used in this country.

Linnæus disposed all plants in twenty-four divisions, each of which is called a CLASS, and each class he subdivided into ORDERS. The first eleven classes are distinguished by the number of separate stamens in each flower.—But tell me, whether you recollect what the stamens and pistils are?

EDWARD.

I think you said, that the whitish threads called

filaments, and the yellow heads, or anthers, were both together the stamens; and the thicker thread, that stands in the middle of them, the pistil.

MOTHER.

You are quite right. I am very glad to find that you remember so well what I tell you.

In the first class, MONANDRIA, each flower contains one stamen.

In the second, DIANDRIA, two stamens; and so on, to the tenth class, DECANDRIA, which has ten stamens in each flower.

In the eleventh class, DODECANDRIA, each flower contains from eleven to nineteen stamens.

In the twelfth, ICOSANDRIA, there are twenty stamens or more in each flower, (the precise number not being of any consequence;) and they are fixed to the calyx.

The thirteenth class, POLYANDRIA, at first sight is like the twelfth; but the difference (which is very important) is, that the stamens are fastened to the receptacle, instead of growing from the sides of the calyx. If you do not perceive this difference at once, on looking at plants of these two classes, the surest way is to pull off gently the calyx, and then, if the stamens remain, you may conclude that they grow upon the receptacle, and that the plant is in the class Polyandria.

The character of the fourteenth class, DIDY-

NAMIA, is, that the flowers have each four stamens, two of them long and two short.

In the flowers of the fifteenth class, TETRADYNAMIA, there are six stamens, four long and two short.

In the sixteenth, MONADELPHIA, the filaments are all united together, forming a little tube round the pistil.

In the flowers of the seventeenth class, DIADELPHIA, the filaments are united at the bottom, generally in two sets.

The eighteenth class, POLYADELPHIA, contains those plants, which have their filaments united at the bottom into three or more little parcels or bundles; as you may see in the large Saint John's-wort in the garden.

The anthers in the nineteenth class, SYNGENESIA, are united, and form a little tube, but the filaments are separate.

In the twentieth class, GYNANDRIA, the stamens grow out of the pistil itself.

The twenty-first class, MONOECIA, contains those plants, in which the stamens and pistils grow in separate flowers, but on the same plant.

The twenty-second, DIOECIA, those in which the stamens and pistils grow in separate flowers, and on different plants.

In the twenty-third class, POLYGAMIA, three different sorts of flowers grow on the same plant;

that is to say, some having pistils only, some stamens only, and others both together.

But Dr. Withering, in his "Arrangement of British Plants," (which is one of the best books that you can refer to, until you have learned Latin,) has distributed the plants of these last four classes, among the first nineteen, according to the number of their stamens.

Those that belong to the twenty-fourth class, CRYPTOGAMIA, have flowers which are not visible to the naked eye; such as ferns, mosses, sea-weeds, mushrooms, &c.

EDWARD.

I am afraid I shall never remember the distinctions of all these classes.

MOTHER.

Do not be alarmed, my dear; here is a drawing I have made (PLATE 2.), that will assist your memory, and show you their different characters; and I have written the Latin names over each figure, that you may learn them as well as the numbers, because they are used by all botanists in speaking of the classes.

EDWARD.

Then how can I learn botany, without knowing Latin?

LATE 2

TABLE OF

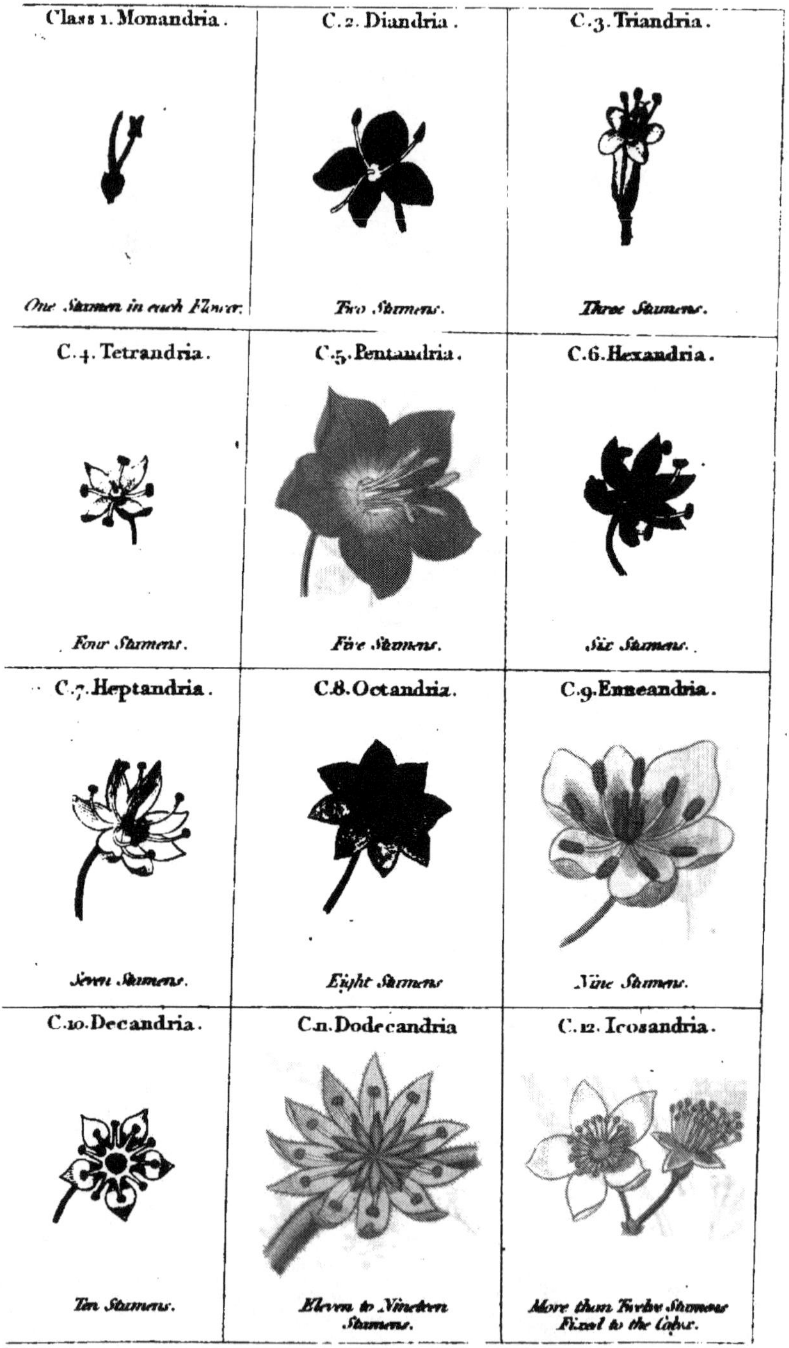

lton sc

Published April 2. 1817 by Longman & Co

THE CLASSES. PLATE 2.

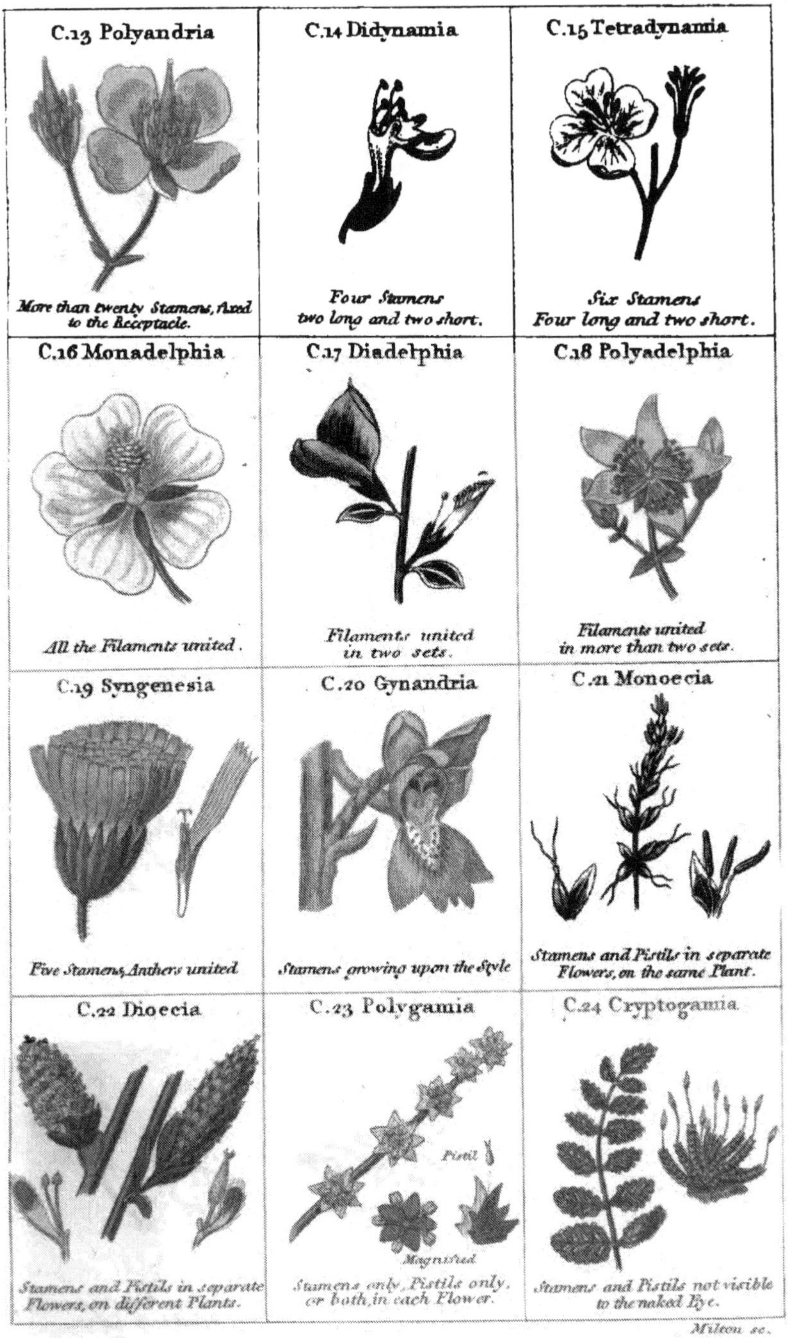

Milton sc.

Published April 2.1817. by Longman &C.°

MOTHER.

It is not necessary to understand Latin generally in order to learn botany, for all the words used in this science are very clearly explained in several botanical works*; and until you are able to make use of those books without my assistance, I will explain every thing as we go on.

EDWARD.

Will you now tell me something about the orders, mamma?

MOTHER.

In the first thirteen classes, from Monandria to Polyandria, the orders are known by the number of Pistils in each flower.

When there is only one pistil, the plant is said to be in the order MONOGYNIA.

If there are two, DIGYNIA.

If three, TRIGYNIA.

If four, TETRAGYNIA.

If five, PENTAGYNIA.

If six, which is not common, HEXAGYNIA.

If seven, HEPTAGYNIA; still less common.

If eight, which scarcely ever occurs, OCTAGYNIA.

If nine, of which there is hardly an instance, ENNEAGYNIA.

If ten, DECAGYNIA.

* Martyn's Language of Botany, &c.

If about twelve, DODECAGYNIA.

Many pistils, POLYGYNIA.

In the 14th class, Didynamia, the orders, which are two, depend upon the the seeds being contained in seed-vessels or not. They are called

GMYNOSPERMIA, when the seeds are naked, or to be seen without a covering; and

ANGIOSPERMIA, when the seeds are enclosed in a seed-vessel.

The orders of the 15th class, Tetradynamia, are also two, and are determined by the shape of the seed-vessels, which are called Pods.

The first has broad short pods, and is called SILICULOSA.

The second has long pods, and is named SILIQUOSA.

In the 16th, 17th, and 18th classes, Monadelphia, Diadelphia, and Polyadelphia, the orders are known by the number of Stamens.

The 19th class, Syngenesia, contains five orders; but as they are rather difficult to understand, it will be time enough to learn them when you come to examine plants of that class, which I should not advise you to do, for some time. Nor is it necessary for you to learn at present the orders of the five remaining classes, which are also difficult.

EDWARD.

I should like to try to find out by myself what class and order some plant belongs to.

MOTHER.

That is the best thing you can do now, and here is a Tulip to begin with. It is always a good way, when you find a plant that is new to you, to examine some of the flowers which are not yet quite opened, as well as those that are; for the anthers are then more distinct, and you may be sure that none of them have been lost.

EDWARD.

I think this tulip is in the sixth class, Hexandria, and the order Monogynia.

MOTHER.

It is, my dear; but why do you think so?

EDWARD.

Because it has six stamens and one pistil. But the anthers are black, instead of yellow like those of the wall-flower that we examined yesterday.— Does that make any difference?

MOTHER.

No. The powder with which the anthers are covered, and which is called Pollen, or Farina, is of different colours in different plants.

EDWARD.

I wish the tulip had a sweet smell, it looks so pretty.

MOTHER.

We must not expect to find in plants any more than in other things, many perfections united, — those that look best are seldom the most useful. — Do you remember the lines our friend wrote for you the other day?

EDWARD.

I believe I do ——

For brilliant tints, to strike the eye,
What plant can with the Tulip vie;
Yet no delicious scent it yields,
To cheer the garden or the fields.
In vain in gaudy colours drest,
'Tis rather gazed at than caress'd.

MOTHER.

I must now finish what I was going to say, before we take our walk.

Linnæus further divided the Classes and Orders into what are called Genera, and these genera again into Species.

A Genus (which is the singular of the word Genera) is formed of a number of plants, that agree with each other in the structure of their flowers and fruit.

A Species includes such plants as agree in these particulars, but differ in others; as in the leaves, the stem, the root, or other parts besides the flower. For instance, in green-houses you often see a great many different sorts of Geranium; these Geraniums form a genus or family of plants, and each different sort is a species of that genus; so that when you hear a person say, an ivy-leaved geranium, an otto-of-rose geranium, or an apple-geranium, you know that they all belong to the genus Geranium, and that the ivy-leaved, &c. are the different species.

In distinguishing plants, two words are always employed by botanists; the first, which is applied to all the species of the same genus, is called the Generic name; but the second is confined to a single species only, and is called the Trivial name. This mode of naming plants is so much approved of, that it is universally used, even by those Botanists who arrange them in a different manner from Linnæus. The two names thus employed are understood in every part of the world, by those who study botany; but the common names are different in different countries. If you were to talk of Wall-flower, or Stock-Gilliflower, to a French or German botanist, he would not understand you, nor would you know what he meant by the French or German names of those plants, though very common in his own country; but the names Cheiranthus fruticulo'sus, and Cheiranthus sinua'tus, would immediately signify to him that you were speaking of two different species of the genus Cheiranthus; and if he did not know them, he could find their descriptions by referring to botanical books.

EDWARD.

Shall we examine a geranium first, as we have so many in our green-house?

MOTHER.

No, my dear, for the genus is in the sixteenth class, Monadelphia; and, I think, it will be easier for you to begin with a plant in one of the first ten classes, which depend on the *number* only of the stamens. Besides, the geraniums in the green-house are not natives of England, that is, they do not grow wild in the hedges and fields; and we shall confine ourselves, for some time, to the examination of native plants only. Although these are generally called weeds, many of them are so beautiful that they are cultivated in flower-gardens. A knowledge of the plants of our own country is more desirable for you than that of foreign ones, as it is more within your reach: and it will be impossible to be thoroughly acquainted with both, unless you devote much more time to the study, than you can give it without neglecting your other employments.

CONVERSATION THE THIRD.

CLASS 1. MONANDRIA. — MARE'S-TAIL. — GLASS-WORT. — INDIAN ARROW-ROOT. — TURMERIC. — CLASS 2. DIANDRIA. — VERONICA CHAMÆDRYS, GERMANDER SPEEDWELL, EXAMINED. — PRIVET. — PEPPER. — ASH-TREE. — OLIVE.

EDWARD.

Mamma, shall we find plants of all the first ten classes in our walks?

MOTHER.

I do not think we shall, for there are very few native plants in the classes Monandria, Heptandria, and Enneandria, (the 1st, 7th, and 9th,) and they are not common. But all that I wish you to do at present is, to gain such a knowledge of the different parts of plants, with their classes and orders, as will enable you to understand and make use of the books which are generally employed by persons who study botany. Even if we did find a plant in the class Monandria, I should not advise you to examine it, as the flowers are very small, and not easily distinguished by a young beginner.

The Mare's-tail, to which Linnæus has given the generic name of Hippu'ris, and the specific name vulga'ris, is in this first class: it grows in muddy ponds, though not very commonly found; and the structure of its flowers, which are very small, and grow close to the stem at the bottom of the leaf, is very simple; for they have no blossom, and only one stamen, one pistil, and one seed. (See PLATE 2. Class 1.)

EDWARD.

But how can it be called a flower without having a blossom?

MOTHER.

All the parts that are necessary to form a perfect flower are the stamens and pistils, for these alone are concerned in the production of the seed. You will find, hereafter, that some flowers have not any calyx, and others no petals (which, you recollect, form the blossom); but you will never find any without stamens or pistils.

If we were near the sea, I could, perhaps, show you an useful plant, the Jointed-Glasswort, or Marsh Samphire, Salicornia herba'cea, which is also in the class Monandria. It has a saltish taste and cattle are very fond of it. In some countries this plant, with several others that grow near the coast, is cut down towards the end of summer, when fully grown; and being dried in the sun, they are burnt for the sake of their ashes, which are used in making glass and soap, and are called kelp.

The Indian Arrow-root too, that your little brother has sometimes for breakfast, is obtained from a plant of this class, Maranta arundina'cea; which is a native of South-America, and has its English name from being supposed to extract the poison from wounds given by the poisoned arrows of the Indians. It has a thick fleshy root, which, when washed, pounded, and bleached, makes the powder that we use as food.

The Turmeric, so commonly used in dyeing yellow, is the root of a plant, called Cur'cuma longa by Linnæus, and is also in the same class. It is very much cultivated in the East-Indies and in China, for the sake of its roots, which are sold in our shops as a dye. But I dare say you are now anxious to examine a plant yourself, so let us go into the fields and look for one.

EDWARD.

Oh, here is a nice little blue flower; shall I take it home, it is so pretty?

MOTHER.

Do, my dear; and if you can tell me the class and order it belongs to, I will show you how to find out its name, in Withering's Botany.

EDWARD.

I see only two stamens, and one pistil; so that,

I suppose, it is in the second class, and the first order. Am I right?

MOTHER.

Yes, perfectly right; but you must remember, if you can, to call each class and order by the names Linnæus gave them.

EDWARD.

Then this plant is in the class Diandria, and the order Monogynia. What am I to do next?

MOTHER.

You must now hold the flower in your hand, and look at every part very attentively, while I read to you the descriptions of a few genera in the class Diandria. The first genus described has a very small cup of one leaf, (that is, consisting of one piece,) with four blunt teeth, or divisions, in its rim. Look at your calyx, and see if it is like this — (See PLATE 3.)

EDWARD.

It is of one piece, but the divisions are sharp.

MOTHER.

Very well. Now look again at your flower. "The blossom of one petal" —

EDWARD.

It cannot be that: for mine has four petals.

MOTHER.

Pull them out, and let me see. I think you will find, that when you attempt to take one, they will all come off together.

EDWARD.

So they do; — and the stamens with them!

MOTHER.

Then you see that your blossom has but one petal, with four divisions, though at first you thought it had four petals. Blossoms formed of one piece, are called Monopetalous, those of many pieces Polypetalous. In flowers of one petal, the stamens are generally fastened to the blossom, and in those of more petals, to the receptacle or calyx; so that in the latter case we may take away the petals without the stamens. This observation affords an easy and pretty certain rule for knowing whether a corolla consists of one petal, or of several, when it is difficult, as it sometimes is, to know this immediately. —We must now go on with our description where we left off.

"The blossom of one petal, shaped somewhat like a funnel; tube of the blossom longer than the cup, — (the tube is the lower part of a blossom of one petal, which stands in the calyx.) — Border of the blossom, (that is, the upper spreading part,) divided into four egg-shaped segments or divisions. Filaments opposite to each other. Anthers nearly as long as the blossom. The germen of the pistil nearly round; style very short; summit thick, blunt, cloven, (that is, divided half-way down). — Does this agree with your plant?

EDWARD.

I think it is something like it, except in the pistil. The summit of mine is not divided, and the style is not very short.

MOTHER.

Well, let us see if the next genus will answer better. — "Calyx, one leaf, with two divisions. Blossom two petals." — We need not go any farther with this, as your flower has but one petal; we must therefore try another: — "Calyx, a cup, with four divisions, each of them sharp. Blossom of one petal; tube of the blossom, nearly as long as the cup; border flat, divided into four egg-shaped parts; the lowest division narrower than any of the others. Stamens two; filaments thinner at the bottom than in the other parts. Anthers oblong. Germen compressed or flattened; style, thread-shaped, as long as the stamens; summit undivided."

PLATE 3

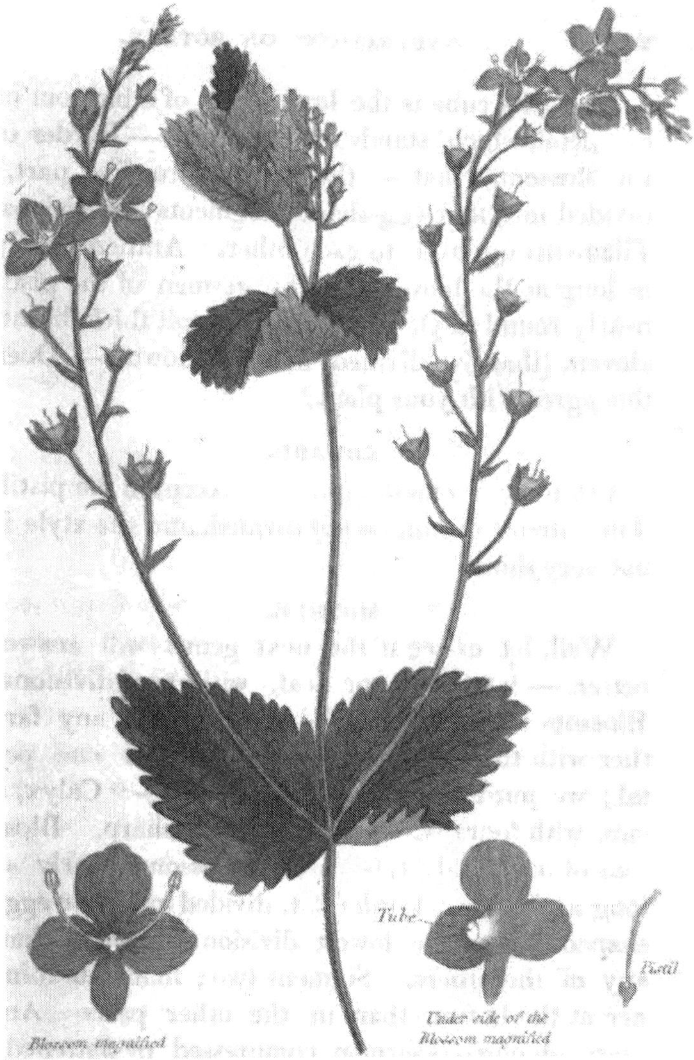

Veronića Chamædrys _ *Germander Speedwell.*

Class II. *DIANDRIA* _ Order *MONOGYNIA.*

Milton sc

[illegible] April 1817 by Longman & Co

EDWARD.

That is exactly like mine, in every thing.

MOTHER.

It is your plant, my dear; so that we need not read any more at present. The genus is called Veroni'ca, and is distinguished from all other genera of the same class and order, by having the lowest division of the blossom narrower than the rest. We ought now to determine what species of Veroni'ca your plant belongs to, by comparing it with the different descriptions given by Withering; but as there are a great many species, and some of them very like each other, I will tell you which it is at once, that you may not be too much puzzled. It is Veroni'ca chamæ'drys, called in English, germander speedwell; [see PLATE 3.] and is known from the other species by the bunches of flowers rising from the sides of the main stem. The leaves are egg-shaped, wrinkled, toothed at the edges, and sitting, (that is, growing close to the stem without any little stalks of their own,) and the stem has two rows of hair, which grow alternately between the joints, on opposite sides.

EDWARD.

I never thought it could be so easy to find out the name of a plant. How plain the description is! — But what was the first plant that you read about, which had the summit divided?

MOTHER.

It was common privet, Ligustrum vulga're, of which hedges are often made, as its grows very fast. The purple colour upon cards is prepared from its berries; which are filled with a spongy violet-coloured pulp, and make also a good green dye, with the addition of alum.

EDWARD.

Are there many useful plants in the class Diandria?

MOTHER.

Not so many as in several of the other classes, but I will mention a few of them.

The black pepper plant, Piper ni'grum, is a native of the East and West Indies, and some of the South-Sea Islands. It is cultivated with such success in the Molucca Islands, Java and Sumatra, that it is exported from them to every part of the world where regular trade is carried on. The white pepper was formerly thought to be a different species from the black; but it is nothing more than the ripe berries deprived of their skin by steeping them in water, after which they are dried in the sun. It is this berry, ground into powder, that you see used every day at dinner.

The common ash, Frax'inus excelsior *, is a native of England; and is placed by Withering in the class Diandria, because the flowers contain two stamens. In the north of Lancashire, when grass is scarce, the tops of the ash trees are cut down to feed the cattle. The wood is hard and tough, and is much used for making tools employed in husbandry.

The olive tree belongs to the genus O'lea, in this class, of which there are several species. It is supposed to have come originally from Asia, where it gave the name to the Mount of Olives near Jerusalem. The O'lea Europæ'a is a small evergreen tree, universally cultivated in the south of Europe for the sake of its fruit, from which olive-oil is obtained by pressing it in a mill. The unripe olives, when pickled, are sent over in barrels to England, where they are eaten at desserts. Another species, called the sweet-scented olive, O'lea fragrans, is kept in green-houses in this country, and is valuable for the delightful scent of its little white flowers, which resembles that of the highest perfumed green tea.

The common lilac, Syrin'ga vulga'ris, a native of Persia, the white jasmine, Jasmi'num officina'le, of the south of Europe, and rosemary, Rosmari'nus

* In the twenty-third class, Polygamia, of Linnæus.

officinalis, an evergreen shrub which grows wild on the shores of the Mediterranean sea, and which you have seen in our garden, are also in the class Diandria, and you will find in them very distinctly the characters of their class and orders. But I am afraid that if I tell you any more at present you will be tired; so we shall leave the third class, Triandria, until to-morrow.

CONVERSATION THE FOURTH.

CLASS 3. — TRIANDRIA. — CROCUS VERNUS, SPRING CROCUS, EXAMINED. — THE GRASSES, — WHEAT, BARLEY, OATS, &c. — SUGAR CANE. — REED. — BAMBOO. — BUTCHERS-BROOM.

EDWARD.

Mamma, will you go out with me now to look for a plant in the third class?

MOTHER.

Yes; but we need not go farther than the garden, for you cannot have a better example than the crocus, which is a native of England, though it does not grow wild in our neighbourhood.

EDWARD.

Here are purple, yellow, and white crocuses; are they of different species?

MOTHER.

Perhaps not; for the character of the species does not depend upon the colour, size, or smell of the flower. Plants which differ in these respects only, are called Varieties: and if you compare these three different coloured crocuses, you will probably find that they agree in the leaves and other parts, which I told you were to be attended to, in distinguishing species. Bring in one of them, and I will read you a description of it. [See PLATE 4.] You perceive that it has three stamens, and one pistil: what class and order then does it belong to?

EDWARD.

To the class Triandria, and order Monogynia.

MOTHER.

Very well. Now look at it as you did at the Veroni'ca: this sort of calyx, which is very different from those I have already described to you, is called a sheath, and is composed of one leaf rising from the stem; and you see it is not green, like the cups of most other flowers, but whitish tinged with brown, and composed of a thin skinny substance. The blossom is of one petal. Tube of the blossom very long: border with six divisions, standing upright, not open and spreading like that of Veroni'ca. Segments egg-shaped, and all of the same size. Stamens three: filaments the shape of an awl, shorter than the blossom; anthers shaped like the head of an arrow. The germen of the pistil, which is placed below the blossom and concealed in the sheath, is roundish; the style thread-shaped; and the summits, which are three in number, are notched like the teeth of a saw, and a little twisted.

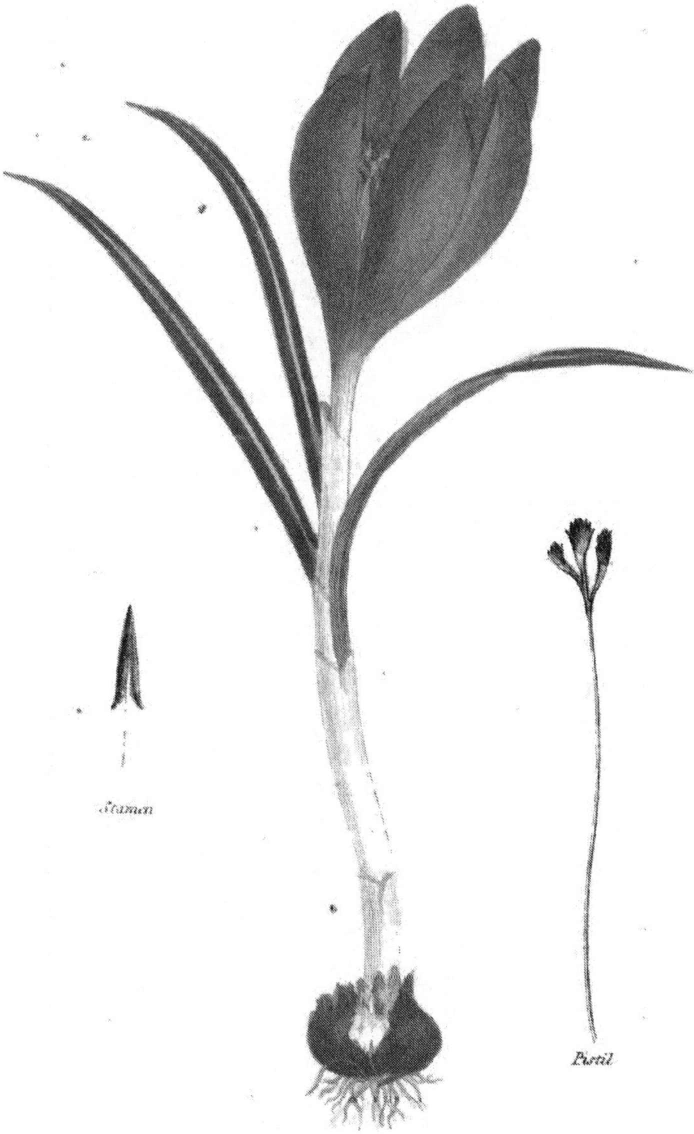

Crócus vérnus _ *Spring Crocus.*

Class III. *TRIANDRIA* _ Order *MONOGYNIA*.

Milton sc.

Published April 2.1817, by Longman & Co.

This is the generic character of Crocus; and our species is the vernus, or spring crocus, which is distinguished by the summits being of a pale colour, not very long, and standing up straight within the flowers.

There are two other native species, sati'vus and nudiflo'rus; but the last is very rare. In the sati'vus, or autumnal saffron, the tube of the blossom is very long, and the summit of the pistil is divided into three long, strap-shaped segments, which are of a full orange colour, and hang out of the blossom. The petals are of a violet colour, and the plant has an agreeable smell. The leaves also, of the saffron, are not so broad as those of the spring crocus.

The summits of the pistil of the Crocus sati'vus, are, I believe, the only parts of any of the species that are made use of. They are carefully picked, pressed together, and dried in kilns, and are then the saffron that is sold in the shops, which was formerly very much used in medicine. There is a place in Essex called Saffron Walden, from the quantity of this plant which was formerly cultivated there, for the purpose of preparing the drug.

EDWARD.

Can we find any other plants of this class in the fields?

MOTHER.

You cannot go into any field without meeting

some of them; for the class Triandria contains almost all the grasses, which are you know so useful: the leaves affording pasture for cattle, the small seeds food for birds, and the larger for men.

EDWARD.

I have never seen the flowers of grasses. Are they pretty?

MOTHER.

I am not surprised that you have never observed them; for, not having petals of brilliant colours like many other flowers, they are generally overlooked; but they are not less curiously constructed than those which are more beautiful in appearance.

The care taken by nature to ensure the production of grass is truly wonderful: Though the leaf be trodden down or consumed, the roots still increase; and the stalks which support the flowers, are seldom eaten by cattle, so that the seeds are always allowed to ripen. The grasses that grow on very high mountains, where the heat is not sufficient to ripen the seed, are propagated by suckers or shoots, which rise from the root, spread along the ground, and then take root themselves.

EDWARD.

But what sort of grass seeds do men eat?

MOTHER.

Wheat, barley, oats, rye, and corn of all kinds,

are the seeds of different grasses. Wheat, Trit'i-cum hybernum, is the grain of which bread is chiefly made. Barley, Hor'deum vulga're, is with us used principally for making beer; but in Spain, where malt liquor is little known, they feed their horses with it, as we do with oats. The poorer people of England, Scotland, and Ireland make use of oats, Ave'na sati'va, ground into meal, for porridge; and in Scotland oaten bread is a common article of food. The inhabitants of Norway make bread of barley and oatmeal, which keeps thirty or forty years; and is even considered as better for being old. At the christening of a child, bread is sometimes made use of, that was baked in the time of its great grandfather.

EDWARD.

Are all these grasses natives of England?

MOTHER.

The particular species which are most valuable, are not native; but we shall find others of the same genera that are.

Couch-grass, the weed that our gardener finds so troublesome, is a species of wheat, Trit'icum re'pens, the roots of which have a sweet taste like liquorice; at Naples, they are sold in the market as food for horses, and are sometimes ground and made into bread.

Wall-barley, Hor'deum muri'num, is a weed very common by road sides, and is eaten by horses and sheep.

The animated oats, that your aunt sometimes amuses you with, are the seeds of the Ave'na fat'ua, which grows wild in corn-fields.

The sea-lime grass, El'ymus arena'rius, which is found pretty commonly on some of our own shores, grows abundantly in Iceland and Greenland, where the climate is too cold to allow the better kinds of corn to ripen; and the seeds are sometimes made into bread by the inhabitants of those miserable countries.

In the island of Rasay, (one of the Scottish Western Isles), the fishermen use ropes for their nets made of the mountain melic-grass, Mel'ica nutans, which grows plentifully there, and is remarkably tough.

The sugar-cane and reed are also grasses. The former, Sac'charum officina'rum, is supposed to have been originally a native of Spain and Sicily, and to have been carried from thence by the Europeans to America and the West-Indies, where it is now very extensively cultivated. The stem, which sometimes grows to the height of twenty feet, affords the juice from whence all our sugar is prepared. You shall read an account this evening of the manner in which it is made.

The sea-reed, Arun'do arena'ria, grows on the

driest sandy parts of our sea-shores, and is so useful in binding the sand, and preventing it from being blown into the neighbouring fields, that Queen Elizabeth forbade the extirpation of it. The Chinese sailors, in rainy weather, use large hats, jackets, and trowsers, made of reeds laid close together, from which the rain runs off, as from the feathers of water-birds.

The bamboo, a native of the East-Indies, is another species of reed, (Arun'do bam'bos of Linnæus), the stalks of which, when young, are almost solid, but as they grow older become hollow, except at the joints: they sometimes measure fifteen inches round, and sixty feet in height, and being strong, durable, and very light, are much used in the construction of buildings, and for making furniture. They serve also in the East for the poles that support a sort of litter or bed, called Palanquin, which is carried about by men, and used like a sedan-chair in this country; only that the palanquin-bearers put the poles upon their shoulders, instead of holding them in their hands like our chairmen. When the joints are bored through, the bamboo is used for water pipes; and walking sticks and fishing-rods are made of the smaller stalks.

EDWARD.

Are not the chairs in your room made in imitation of bamboo?

MOTHER.

They are, except the seats, which are made of bull-rushes, Scir'pus lacus'tris, a plant of this class, that grows abundantly in clear ditches and streams in England. Cottages are sometimes thatched with these rushes, and cattle eat them when other food is scarce.

EDWARD.

I should like to examine some of the grasses, they seem to be so useful.

MOTHER.

When you know more of botany, you may do so, my dear; but there are so many of them, that I should advise you to confine yourself at first to other plants, and leave the grasses for a separate study at some other time.

Besides the crocus and the grasses, there are several other plants in this class, which you will find growing wild. Do you remember how much pleased you were last winter, in Devonshire, with the plant in the woods, that had the pretty little flowers growing on the middle of the leaves?

EDWARD.

Oh yes! and it had beautiful red fruit, that looked like cherries, What was the name of it?

MOTHER.

Butchers-broom, Ruscus aculea'tus. It is also in the class Triandria of Withering's arrangement; but as the stamens and pistils are not in the same flowers, nor even upon the same plants, Linnæus has placed this genus in the twenty-second class, Dioecia. In general the berries are not larger than black currants, but the warmth of the climate in Devonshire increases their size. In Italy, the plant is made into brooms, which the butchers use for sweeping their blocks; and from this circumstance it has obtained its English name.

CONVERSATION THE FIFTH.

CLASS 4.—TETRANDRIA.—ILEX AQUIFOLIUM, COMMON HOLLY, EXAMINED.—CLOTHIERS TEASEL.—MADDER.—BIRCH TREE.—ALDER.—DUTCH MYRTLE.—BOX.—CENTUNCULUS MINIMUS.—MISELTOE.—PARASITICAL PLANTS.—EPIDENDRUM FLOS-AËRIS.

MOTHER.

Well Edward, if you are inclined to begin the fourth class, Tetrandria, to-day, bring me a piece of holly from the garden, and we will compare it with the description.

EDWARD.

Is holly a native plant, mamma?

MOTHER.

Yes, one of the species grows wild in England: The botanical name is Ilex aquifolium; and it is in the order Tetragynia of this class.

EDWARD.

I thought that all the leaves of holly were prickly, but here are some quite smooth.

MOTHER.

It has been observed, I think by Linnæus, that

the lower branches, within the reach of cattle, bear thorny leaves, while the upper ones, which do not want a defence, are without thorns.

EDWARD.

But would cattle eat them if they had no thorns?

MOTHER.

They would; and in winter, when other food is scarce, the upper boughs, that have smooth leaves, are sometimes cut down, and strewed upon the ground to feed deer and sheep. They peel off the bark also very nicely, and eat it with the smooth leaves.

EDWARD.

Will you now read the description of the holly, while I look at the flower?

MOTHER.

In the genus Ilex, [see PLATE 5.] the calyx is a very small cup, which has four or five teeth at the edge. The blossom is of one petal, generally with four divisions, but there is some variety in this respect. The segments roundish and spreading out. The stamens are four, and shorter than the blossom. The germen is roundish; and there are four summits, but no styles. The seed-vessel is a roundish berry, containing four very hard seeds. The leaves in our species, aquifolium, are egg-shaped, thorny, and evergreen, surrounded by a thickened border; and, in the tree from which this specimen was taken, they are what is called variegated; the leaves in the wild state not being stained with white, but of an uniform dark green colour. The berries are of a bright scarlet.

EDWARD.

I do not understand what is meant by evergreen?

MOTHER.

Those plants that retain their green leaves all the year, in winter as well as in summer, are called so.

The wood of the holly is remarkably white and hard, and takes a fine polish. It is chiefly used by inlayers and engravers on wood, and some of the pretty Tunbridge ware is made of it.

I will now tell you of a few other plants in the class Tetrandria. The clothier's teasel, Dip'sacus fullo'num, is very much cultivated in the west of England, and is of the greatest value in cloth manufactories. The heads of flowers are fastened round the edge of a large broad wheel, which is kept turning, while the cloth is held against them, and the crooked awns, with which they are furnished, raise the knap on the cloth.

EDWARD.

What are the awns?

Ílex Aquifólium — *Common Holly.*

Class IV. *TETRANDRIA* — Order *TETRAGYNIA.*

Milton sc.

Published April 1. 1817, by Longman & Co.

MOTHER.

They are slender, sharp bristles, such as you see growing from the husks of barley and oats, and which you call the beard. In this species of teasel, they are stiff, strong, and hooked backwards at the ends; which is the reason that the plant is so useful to clothiers.

There is another plant (called dyer's madder, Ru'bia tincto'rum), common in the west of England, the root of which affords a very beautiful scarlet dye; but what is cultivated in Holland is considered by dyers as better than that of other countries. Madder has the property of tinging with its red colour, the milk, and even the bones of the animals that feed upon it.

The white birch, Bet'ula alba, (in this class, according to Withering*,) is very useful to the inhabitants of the north of Europe: it endures the severity of cold climates better than any other tree; and the seeds, which are furnished with little wings, are often carried by the winds to the tops of buildings, and of high rocks, where they take root and grow. The sap or juice obtained from the trunk in spring, is said to make a pleasant wine, with the addition of sugar; and in the northern parts of Lancashire, the young

* In class 21, Monoecia of Linnæus.

twigs are made into brooms, which are exported to different countries. The bark has the singular property of being more firm and durable than the wood itself. A French traveller*, in passing through Lapland, where there are vast forests of birch, observed, upon examining the trees which had been blown down by the storms, that in several instances the wood was entirely gone; the trunks, though to all appearance solid, consisting only of a shell of bark. In Norway, Sweden, and Russia, this bark is cut into square pieces like tiles, to cover the roofs of the houses; the Swedish fishermen make shoes of it; the inhabitants of Kamschatka, hats and drinking cups; and the people of Canada, canoes.

The inner silky bark of the birch was used for writing on, before the invention of paper.

The alder tree, which you may see on the banks of rivers, is another species of Bet'ula, the Alnus, the wood of which is soft and brittle, but lasts a long time under water, and is therefore used for water-pipes, and for beams to lay under the foundations of buildings situated in marshy places.

The Dutch myrtle, Myri'ca ga'le, which is found in our bogs, is in the class Tetrandria, according to Withering.† The flowers grow in little

* M. Maupertuis.

† In the 22d class Dioecia, and order Tetrandria, of Linnæus.

clusters, which are called catkins; and when these are boiled in water, they throw up a scum like bee's-wax, that would make candles if collected in sufficient quantity. In America, candles, soap, and sealing-wax, are actually made from another species, called candle-berry myrtle, Myri'ca cerif'era.

The common box, Buxus sempervi'rens, with which part of our garden is bordered, is also placed by Withering in the fourth class.* It is an evergreen, and the slowest growing of all our trees, which renders its wood particularly hard, and of a fine close texture, and therefore very valuable for mathematical instruments, and the finer kinds of turner's ware, that require wood of a smooth grain. The beautiful engravings of animals and birds, by Bewick, are cut upon this wood. In the south of Europe, the box-tree is kept in flower-pots, with as much care as we bestow upon myrtle. You have seen only small trees, but it grows in great abundance, to the height of ten or twelve feet, at Box-hill, in Surrey.

EDWARD.

Will our borders ever grow so high?

MOTHER.

No; what is used for garden-borders is a dwarf, or a very small variety (but not a different species) of the plant that I have just mentioned.

* In the class Monoecia, and order Tetrandria, of Linnæus.

EDWARD.

How did you find out so many curious things about plants?

MOTHER.

By reading different botanical works and books of travels, which I will lend you when you are old enough to understand them; but you will find that I know very little, indeed almost nothing, of the subject, in comparison with many other persons, and less than you yourself can easily learn hereafter. I hope that if ever you become a good botanist, you will still recollect the lines that you heard sung last night: —

What though I trace each herb and flower,
That drinks the morning dew;
Did I not own Jehovah's power,
How vain were all I knew!

But there are some other plants of the fourth class, that I must not forget; — the pimpernel chaffweed, Centun'culus min'imus, the smallest of all the British plants that have distinct flowers, the stem being hardly an inch high; and several parasitical plants.

EDWARD.

What does that mean?

* In the 22d class of Linnæus.

MOTHER.

Parasitical plants are those which are produced upon the trunks, branches, or any parts of other vegetables, and which, in some instances, will not grow in the ground, as is the case with miseltoe, and some kinds of funguses. The miseltoe, Viscum album *, is an evergreen shrub, that grows in great perfection on apple trees. Nobody has ever yet succeeded in making it take root in the earth, but if the berries, when fully ripe, are rubbed on the smooth bark of almost any tree, they will adhere closely, and produce plants the following winter.

There are parasites of another kind, less properly called so, which at first take root in the ground, and afterwards fasten themselves to trees, or other substances within their reach, where they strike out roots from their own stems.

EDWARD.

Then, I suppose, ivy is a parasitical plant?

MOTHER.

Yes, it is one of those I have just mentioned; and you shall hear more about it, when we come to the fifth class, to which it belongs. But some of the most remarkable native parasites are of the genus Cus'cuta, or Dodder, in the second order of this class: they have no leaves, but only a slender stalk, with which they lay hold very closely of some

* In the 22d class, Diœcia, of Linnæus.

plant stronger than themselves, from whence they draw all their nourishment. There are five native species, which grow upon beans, hops, flax, heath, and the nettle; frequently in such profusion as to destroy the plant that supports them.

There is a parasitical genus peculiar to hot climates, the Epidendrum *, one species of which, called Flos a'ëris, (or flower of the air,) is particularly curious. It is found in abundance in the East Indies, beyond the river Ganges, and it grows and even blossoms in the air, when hung up, without attaching itself to any solid body. The smell of the flowers is so delightful, that the inhabitants suspend it from the cielings of their rooms, where it will vegetate for years. †

Parasitical plants have been lately discovered, which grow upon others that are themselves parasites, but they are very rare.

* In the 20th class, Gynandria, of Linnæus.
† Willdenow's "Principles of Botany," p. 265.

CONVERSATION THE SIXTH.

CLASS 5. — PENTANDRIA. — GENUS SOLANUM, POTATOE. — WOODY AND GARDEN NIGHTSHADE. — DEADLY NIGHTSHADE, A DIFFERENT GENUS. — ATROPA. — IVY. — BUCKTHORN. — MYOSOTIS PALUSTRIS, WATER MOUSE-EAR, EXAMINED. — VINE. — CURRANT AND GOOSEBERRY. — COFFEE TREE.

MOTHER.

THE fifth class, Pentandria, comprehends more than a tenth part of all the plants that are known at present; and some of our most useful vegetables belong to it. I shall begin with the potatoe, Sola'num tubero'sum, which is in theorder Monogynia.

EDWARD.

Do potatoes grow wild in England?

MOTHER.

No; they are said to have been brought from America, by Sir Walter Raleigh, who, on his return from that part of the world, about the year 1597, distributed a number of potatoes in Ireland, where they were planted, and multiplied very fast. They were afterwards brought from thence into England; and a ship, laden with potatoes, being wrecked on the coast of Lancashire, the cultivation of them soon became general. It is remarkable that Virginia, the country which is supposed to have afforded the potatoes first brought to Europe, was afterwards saved from famine by a supply of them from Ireland.

Go and ask the gardener for some of the blossoms, and you will see that they are in the first order of the fifth class: you already know that what we eat is a part of the root.

EDWARD.

Here is one bunch with white, and another with purple flowers. Are they only varieties?

MOTHER.

That is all, my dear; the plants with white flowers are said to have white roots, and those with purple, red ones.

EDWARD.

And these little green balls; are they the seeds?

MOTHER.

They are the seed-vessels, and contain the seeds within them. If the seeds of any one plant were sown, they would produce a great many varieties of potatoes; but in general this vegetable is propagated by the roots, which ensures the production of plants of the same quality.

Look at the anthers, and you will perceive that

they are nearly united at top in a point, and that there are two little holes in each of them; this is what constitutes the principal distinguishing character of the genus Sola'num, of which there are more than three hundred species; but only two of them are natives of England, the dulcama'ra and ni'grum. You will, perhaps, be surprised to hear that the woody nightshade, which grows wild in our hedges, and bears the pretty scarlet berries that I have so often told you were poisonous, belongs to the same genus as the potatoe: it is the Sola'num dulcama'ra.

The garden nightshade, Sola'num ni'grum, is also poisonous: and even the smell of it is said to occasion sleep: the flowers are white, and the ripe berries black. The Deadly nightshade is another plant in the same class and order, and from its English name, you might suppose it to be of the same genus also; but its flower is very different: this will show you how necessary it is to use the botanical names, in speaking of plants to botanists.

EDWARD.

What then is the botanical name of Deadly nightshade?

MOTHER.

At'ropa belladon'na. It grows wild in Europe, particularly in England and Austria; and every part of it is poisonous.

The Tomato, or love apple, that you often see in fruit shops, is the Sola'num lycoper'sicum; the berry is about the size of a plum, and is used in soups. In Jamaica, another species, the Sola'num melonge'na, is very much cultivated, and is called the egg-plant, or vegetable-egg, from the fruit, which in shape and size is very like the egg of a hen.

Our common ivy, Hed'era he'lix, is also in the same class and order, Pentandria Monogynia. It is the only native species of Hed'era, and is the latest flowering of all our plants, for it blossoms in October and November; but the berries are not ripe until the following spring.

EDWARD.

But, are there not two kinds of ivy growing on the old church?

MOTHER.

Although the leaves are different, they belong in reality to the same species. When the common ivy trails on the ground, the branches are small and weak, and the leaves have three divisions; but when it climbs up walls or trees, the plant grows much stronger, and the figure of the leaf is changed to egg-shaped.

The buckthorn, Rhamnus cathar'ticus, which belongs likewise to this class and order, grows wild in woods and hedges in various parts of Europe.

The unripe fruit is sold under the name of French berries, and affords a juice that is used for staining maps and paper yellow. The juice of the ripe berries, mixed with alum, forms the sap-green employed by painters; and if the berries are gathered late in autumn, their juice is purple. The bark of the stem dyes a beautiful yellow colour. The unripe fruit of another species, the yellow-berried buckthorn, Rhamnus infecto'rius, a native of the south of Europe, is said to give the yellow colour to Turkey or Morocco leather.

In Africa, the negroes make bread of a sweet yellow berry, the fruit of the Rhamnus lo'tus, which they call Tomberongs. When the berries are dried, they pound them into meal, and make cakes of it, which, when dried in the sun, have the colour and taste of gingerbread.

EDWARD.

Shall we not examine a plant to-day?

MOTHER.

Yes, certainly: To examine plants is the best way to learn botany. Here is a piece of water-mouse-ear, Myoso'tis palus'tris. [See PLATE 6.] Tell me its class and order.

EDWARD.

I do not see any stamens; where are they?

MOTHER.

Pull off one of the blossoms, and cut it open with your pen-knife.

EDWARD.

Now I do see five stamens; but the anthers are almost covered by the little yellow parts, that met in the middle before I opened it.

MOTHER.

These form one of the characters of the genus Myoso'tis:—but you have not told me the order?

EDWARD.

It is the first, Monogynia, for I see only one pistil, which has remained in the calyx.

MOTHER.

Very well. The calyx is a cup with five sharp oblong divisions: the blossom is of one petal; the border has five blunt divisions, very slightly notched at the ends; the mouth, or upper part of the tube, is closed with five small projecting parts, called valves: the stamens are placed in the neck of the tube, and the filaments are very short; the anthers small, and covered by the valves. The style is as long as the tube of the blossom. There is no seed-vessel, but the cup enlarges as the seeds ripen, and contains them within it. In this species,

Myosótis palustris _ *Water Mouse Ear.*

Class V. *PENTANDRIA* __ Order *MONOGYNIA*.

Myoso'tis palus'tris, the leaves are spear-shaped, the seeds smooth, and the calyx funnel-shaped, with straight and close-pressed hairs.

EDWARD.

I think I shall always know mouse-ear, when I see it, from the little valves in the middle of the blossom.

MOTHER.

These do form one of the principal characters of the genus: but you must attend besides to the other circumstances that I have mentioned; for there are other genera of the same classs and order, which are also furnished with valves.

The vine, Vi'tis, is a genus of this class. The common species, vinif'era, which produces grapes, is a native of the south of Europe, where a great many varieties are cultivated, from which different kinds of wine are obtained. The fruit, you know, is generally produced in hot-houses in this part of England; but it grows and ripens very well in the open air in some of the southern counties.

The currant and gooseberry are also in the class Pentandria, and order Monogynia. Their generic name is Ri'bes.

EDWARD.

Then are currants and gooseberries of the same

genus?—They look very different from each other.

MOTHER.

When you examine the flowers, you will find that they agree in character. In the little yellowish flowers of a currant or gooseberry-bush, you will see that each has five petals, which, as well as the stamens, are fixed to the calyx: the style is cloven: and the blossom is superior, that is, it grows above the germen; which afterwards becomes the fruit and contains within it little hard seeds, dispersed through a pulpy substance; as you will find if you open a currant or gooseberry.

There are several species of Ri'bes, some producing different sorts of currants, and others gooseberries. All the currant kind are without thorns, and bear clusters of flowers and fruit: but the branches of the gooseberry, are thorny, and the flowers, in general, solitary; only one growing from the same part of the plant, instead of a bunch.

EDWARD.

Are they all natives of England?

MOTHER.

No; there are not more than six or seven native species; two of gooseberries, and four or five of car-rants. Both fruits succeed very well in our gardens.

It is remarkable, that no thin-skinned fruits, such as grapes, cherries, currants, strawberries, plums, apricots, and peaches, nor even common apples and pears, ever come to perfection in very hot climates; although a greater number of vegetables are calculated to bear a high degree of warmth than to endure cold.

The coffee-tree, is of the genus Coffe'a, in this class and order: the oriental kind, Coffe'a Arab'ica, is a native of Arabia, and a second species, Occidenta'lis, grows in the West Indies. The trees are evergreen, but seldom grow higher than seventeen or eighteen feet. The fruit, which is the only useful part, resembles a small cherry, and when fit to be gathered is of a deep red colour: it contains two seeds, and these, when roasted and ground, are what we make use of. They are collected in large quantities, and sent to all parts of Europe. It is said that coffee was first sold in England about the year 1680, by the servant of a Turkish merchant.

There is another genus in the first order of the fifth class, that you will be glad to hear of: the Violet, Vi'ola.—

EDWARD.

Don't you love violets; they smell so sweet and grow in such pleasant shady places.

MOTHER.

There are five or six other native species, besides your favourite, which is called Vi'ola odora'ta: The heart's-ease or pansies, Vi'ola tric'olor, is one of these, though its flower is so different in appearance from that of the sweet-scented species.

CONVERSATION THE SEVENTH.

CLASS 5. CONCLUDED. — DESCRIPTION OF AN UMBEL. — UMBELLIFEROUS PLANTS. — ELDER. — TEAK WOOD. — FLAX, ITS USES. — PAPER.

MOTHER.

By far the greater part of the order Digynia, in the fifth class, is composed of what are called umbelliferous or umbellate plants, which are so named from their peculiar structure. From the top of a straight stalk there grow several smaller ones, called spokes, which spread out from it, as from a centre, like the wires in the inside of an umbrella when it is open; and the plants are called umbellate, from the word umbella, which is the Latin for an umbrella. Each set of spokes forms what is called an umbel; and every spoke is terminated by an umbellule (or little umbrella,) which consists of a number of smaller stalks, with a single flower at the end of each. You cannot have better examples of this tribe than the common hemlock and garden parsley.

Several of the umbelliferous plants are remarkable for their uses as food or medicine, or else for their poisonous qualities. The roots of most of those which grow in dry soils have an aromatic smell and taste; but in moist situations, or in water, they are nearly all poisonous.

The water cow-bane, Cicu'ta viro'sa, grows in pools and rivers, and is one of the most violent of vegetable poisons. Early in the spring cows are often killed by eating it; but as the summer advances, the smell becomes stronger, and they carefully avoid it. Linnæus mentions, in his *Lapland Tour*, that he was told of a disease amongst the cattle at Torneo, which killed a great many of them in the winter, but was still more prevalent in the spring, when they were first turned out to grass; and which the inhabitants could not account for. On examining the place where the cattle had fed, he found it to be a marsh, in which the Cicu'ta viro'sa grew in abundance; and by pointing out the plant, he enabled the people to guard against the danger ever after.

The water-parsnep, Sium latifo'lium, and water-hemlock, Phellan'drium aquat'icum, both natives of England, are also very poisonous. The carrot, Dau'cus carro'ta; parsnep, Pastina'ca sati'va; angelica, Angel'ica Archangel'ica; carraway, Ca'rum car'ui; coriander, corian'drum sati'vum; and parsley, A'pium grave'olens; most of which you are acquainted with, are all umbelliferous plants, and grow wild in England.

In Poland, the poor people make a fermented drink, which they use instead of ale, from the leaves and seeds of the cow-parsnep, Heraclеum sphondyl'ium, another umbellate plant, which is a troublesome weed in our meadows; and the Kamschatkans and Russians peel its stalks and eat them.

But do you think you can distinguish an umbelliferous plant from any other, by the description that I have given you? Go out, and try if can find one.

EDWARD.

Here, mamma, are two, which I found at the side of the field, next the road.

MOTHER.

You have made a very good attempt, my dear; and are right in one of them, the shepherd's needle, Scandix pecten. I am not surprised at your mistaking the other, which is the common elder, Sambu'cus Eb'ulus, for it certainly has the general appearance of an umbelliferous plant: but if you look again, you will perceive that it has not exactly the structure which I have described to you;

for, though all the principal ribs grow from the same stalk, like those in the umbel of the shepherd's needle, there are no umbellules, the smaller stalks not being regularly arranged.

The character of the umbelliferous tribe, is in part taken from the structure of the flower itself. In umbellate plants, the corolla has five petals, with a stamen between every two: and two styles rise from the centre of the flower, each with a single summit; which remain after the petals and stamens fall off, and crown the two seeds. The calyx, which in this tribe is called an involucrum, is in general not very distinct.

Now look at your elder, and you will see that the blossom, instead of having five petals, is of one piece, divided into five parts: there are, it is true, five stamens; but there is no style; and you will more frequently find three summits than two. The fruit of the elder is a soft berry; but in the umbelliferous tribe, it consists of two dry and naked seeds.

EDWARD.

Why does the gardener spread elder leaves near the mole hills?

MOTHER.

To keep away the moles, which will not come near elder. You may have seen the coachman also putting branches of it in the horses' heads to keep off the flies, for few insects can endure the smell of this plant.

I shall conclude to-day, by telling you something about a few curious foreign trees, and our own useful plant, the flax, which are in the class Pentandria.

The marking-nut tree, Semicar'pus anecar'dium, is a native of woody mountains in the East Indies. It is a lofty tree, and bears a fruit that contains a black resinous juice, which is used in the East for marking linen. This is done by putting the linen over the nut, and pricking it till the juice comes through, which makes a stain that never washes out. The fleshy receptacle, when roasted, has the flavour of apples, and is eaten by the natives of India.

The forests of Java, Ceylon, and some other of the East Indian islands, afford a very valuable tree, called the Indian oak, or teak wood, Tec'tona grandis. The leaves, even on young trees, are nearly two feet long, and more than a foot in breadth. The trunk grows to a great size, and the wood is the most useful timber of the East; it is supposed to be superior to every other for building ships, for the worms that destroy fir and oak, do not injure it.

The common flax, Li'num usitatissimum, in the order Pentagynia of this class, is one of the most valuable of plants; for every kind of linen is manufactured from the bark of its stalks, and linen, worn to rags, makes paper. It is said that the plant came originally from Egypt; but it is now found wild in many parts of England. The seeds afford linseed oil, which is used in great quantities by painters; and after the oil has been pressed out, they form what are called oil cakes, with which cattle are fattened. The linnet has its name from the Li'num, because flax seed is its favourite food. It will interest you very much to read an account of the method of preparing flax for making linen.

EDWARD.

Is all paper made of linen rags?

MOTHER.

No; what we most commonly use in England is so; but there are several other kinds, made of different materials. Paper was first manufactured in Europe about the year 1300, but it is not known by whom it was invented. The Egyptian paper, which was in general use among the ancients, was the inner coat of the stem of the Cy'perus papy'rus, a species of rush, (in the class Triandria,) that grows on the banks of the Nile. In China, paper is prepared from the bark of several different trees;

among others, of the elm and mulberry, but chiefly of the cotton tree. Our blotting paper is made principally of woollen rags. I have seen also paper that was manufactured of silk, straw, sea-weed, and even of leather: this last kind being particularly useful for packing, as it is water-proof, and does not easily tear or take fire.

CONVERSATION THE EIGHTH.

CLASS 6. HEXANDRIA. — GALANTHUS NIVALIS, SNOWDROP, EXAMINED. — NECTARIES. — BARBERRY; ITS FILAMENTS. — SORREL. — INDIAN REED. — LARGE PLANTS OF HOT CLIMATES. — GREAT FAN PALM. — ARISTOLOCHIA. — ADANSONIA. — CLIMBERS. — TERMS EXPLAINED. — LILIES. —BULBOUS ROOTS.—KAMSCHATKA LILY.

EDWARD.

WHAT shall we do to-day, mamma? I hope we shall examine a plant in the sixth class.

MOTHER.

I believe, my dear, that the snowdrop is one of the best examples you can have, for the flower is very remarkable, and the only species which is known, is a native of England.

EDWARD.

But the snowdrop has done flowering long ago.

MOTHER.

Very true: it is one of our earliest spring flowers. You remember Mrs. Barbauld's beautiful lines, which I gave you to learn in February, when you brought me the first snowdrop from the garden.

EDWARD.

Already now the Snowdrop dares appear,
The first pale blossom of the unripen'd year.
As nature's breath by some transforming power,
Had changed an icicle into a flower;
Its name and hue the scentless plant retains,
And winter lingers in its icy veins.

MOTHER.

We cannot then procure a living plant at present; but, I will read you a description of it, which you may compare with this drawing [see PLATE 7.] and you must not forget next spring to examine a real one. The flower has six stamens and one pistil; it is therefore in the class Hexandria, and order Monogynia. There is no cup, but instead of one a sheath, (a kind of calyx, of which this plant affords a very good example;) and there are six petals, three smaller than the rest, standing within the other three, and notched at the ends.

EDWARD.

How very different they are from the other petals!

MOTHER.

For this reason they were considered by Linnæus as distinct from them, and called by him the nectaries. In the snowdrop, these three inner parts of the flower, whether we call them nectaries or petals, form the distinguishing character of the genus, which is named Galanthus.

EDWARD.

But when we were examining the wall-flower, you told me that the nectaries were little bodies surrounding the stamens.

MOTHER.

Yes; but I also told you, that nectaries had different forms in different flowers. The use of the nectary you know is supposed to be, to contain the honey: in monopetalous flowers, the tube of the blossom itself answers this purpose; but in flowers of several petals, with open calyxes, which have no tube to hold it, there is in general a distinct part intended for that use.

In some genera, the nectary is a sort of horn or spur at the back of the flower, as you will see very distinctly in the larkspur and columbines: and there is a genus in the fifth class, called Parnassia, in which the nectaries are particularly beautiful. One species of this genus, the palus'tris, grows wild in England, and exhibits them in great perfection. There are five in every flower, placed alternately between the stamens; and each consists of a little heart-shaped substance, beautifully fringed with bristles; every bristle bearing on its extremity a transparent yellow ball, in appearance like melted wax. Here is a little drawing that will give you some idea of their figure.

PLATE 7

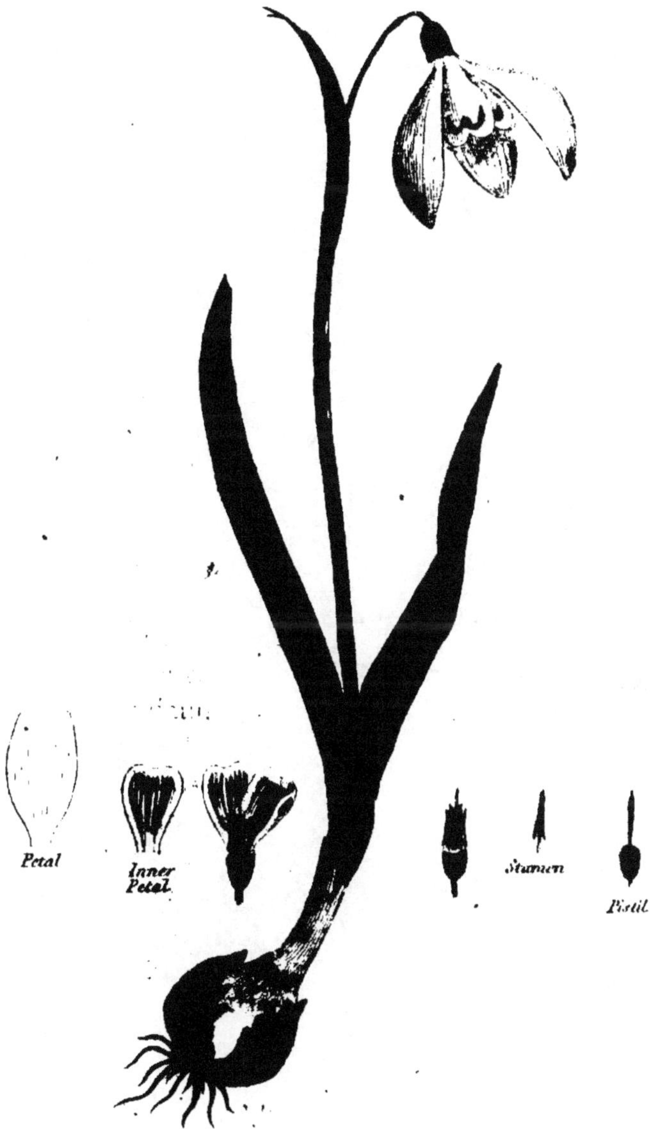

Galanthus nivâlis_*Snowdrop*.

Class VI *HEXANDRIA* _ Order *MONOGYNIA*.

Miller

Published April 1817, by Longman & Co.

But, let us return to our snowdrop. The filaments of the Galan'thus are very short, and the anthers end in a fine point like a bristle. The pistil is longer than the stamens; the style thread-shaped; and the germen is rather large, roundish, and placed below the blossom, so that you can see it without pulling off the petals. The specific name of the snowdrop, is niva'lis.

EDWARD.

You have not described the leaves or the root.

MOTHER.

When there is but one species known of any genus, it is unnecessary to do so. You may recollect, I told you that the character of a genus depended upon the structure of the flower; and that of the species upon the leaves, roots, or other parts. Now as there is but one species of Galan'thus, we do not want a specific description, not having any other to compare it with.

EDWARD.

I like to examine plants that have but one species.

MOTHER.

It certainly is less difficult for a beginner, than when there are many; which is my reason for choosing such plants for you when I can.

You already know that the tulip is in the sixth class. There is one species called wild tulip, Tu'lipa sylves'tris, a native of England. It differs from the garden tulip, Tu'lipa Gesneria'na, which grows wild in the Levant, in having narrow leaves; a flower that nods or bends downwards, and is fragrant: the pollen also, on the anthers of the native species, is yellow instead of black.

The pine-apple, Brome'lia ana'nas, that you see in the hot-house; lily of the valley, Convalla'ria maja'lis; asparagus, Aspar'agus officina'lis; hyacinth, Hyacinthus non-scriptus; and barberry, Ber'beris vulga'ris, are amongst the plants in the first order of the sixth class. They are all natives of England, except the pine-apple, which is said to have come originally from South America; the fruit has its name, from the resemblance of its shape to the cone or seed-vessel of some of the pine trees.

There is one circumstance relating to the barberry, that deserves particular attention. The flowers contain six stamens, each of them fastened by its lower part to one of the petals, which are also six in number. The filaments spread out a little, and the anthers are covered by the upper part of the petals. If any thing, an insect for example in search of honey, touches the filament near the bottom, it immediately contracts, and strikes its anther against the summit of the pistil;

but any other part of the stamen may be touched without producing this effect. In the entire flower, the filament that has contracted, gradually goes back of itself to its original position, and may be made to move as before, several times, without losing this property; and even when the petals fall off with the stamens that are fixed to them, the filament still retains its power of moving.

The berries of the barberry are so very acid, that birds will not eat them; but we use them boiled with sugar as a sweet-meat. The leaves also are acid, and the bark of the root is used in Poland for dyeing leather of a beautiful yellow colour.

Sorrel, Ru'mex aceto'sa, is in the order Trigynia of this class. The Laplanders use it in preparing a kind of whey from rein-deer's milk, which will keep a long time.

EDWARD.

Is this the same kind of sorrel that we sometimes eat, when we gather it in the fields.

MOTHER.

Yes, and it is also used in sallad. In France, another species, Rumex scuta'tus, is cultivated for the table.

The rice plant, Ory'za, is in the order Digynia of this class, but has the form and structure of the grasses, from which it differs only in the number of the stamens. Linnæus was acquainted with but one species, the Ory′za sati′va, but I believe that others have been since discovered. The common rice, a native of India, is cultivated throughout the East, where it is of the first importance to the inhabitants as an article of food.

The Indian reed, Cal′amus petræ′us, is another plant of the same class, which also resembles a grass in some respects; but the stems grow to more than a hundred feet in height, and are then at least the thickness of a man's arm; they are used in Cochin-China for making long pikes; and the inner part of the young shoots is eaten by the natives. Another species of Cal′amus, the ro′tang, or ratan, has very smooth glassy stems, marked with dark spots; and the long spaces between the joints are used for walking canes. It grows abundantly on both sides of the Straits of Malacca, from whence it is sent into Europe. There is a third species, Cal′amus vernus, which is very common in forests in the East Indies: Though not thicker than a man's finger, it often extends to the length of more than a hundred feet, and when split into strips is used for making ropes, seats of chairs, and several articles of furniture.

EDWARD.

How very large the plants in India grow.

MOTHER.

In all hot countries vegetables grow to a great size; and on the contrary the plants of cold climates are very diminutive. The difference of size in going southward from this country, begins to be perceived even in Italy, where the millet (a sort of corn) attains the height of four or five yards. In the East-Indies there is a plant called the Great Fan-palm, Cor'ypha umbraculif'era, with leaves more than six yards in breadth, which grow in the form of an umbrella; and a species of Aristolochia, (class Hexandria, of Withering*,) that grows on the banks of the river La Madalina, in South America, has flowers of such great size, that they are used by the children in play, for hats. Another species of this genus, Aristolo'chia clemati'tis, grows wild in our woods and hedges.

The Monkey's bread-tree, Adanso'nia digita'ta, is found on the banks of the river Senegal in Africa, and has its name from M. Adanson, a French traveller, who resided several years in that country. The stem is only twelve or fifteen feet high, but frequently from eighty to ninety feet in circumference; and the top is crowded with great branches like trees, which run out from it in all directions, and touch the ground at their extremities; the roots often spreading to more than a hundred feet

* In the twentieth class, Gynandria, of Linnæus.

around. You will then not be surprised to hear, that whole families of negroes sometimes live in the hollow trunk of this tree; which is said also to be one of the longest-lived of all trees, and has been computed to live more than a thousand years.

Near the equator, too, gigantic climbers are found, which grow to the length of several hundred yards.

EDWARD.

What are climbers?

MOTHER.

Plants that are unable to support themselves, but take advantage of whatever is near to raise themselves upon, are called by that name; such as the vine, and virgin's bower.

EDWARD.

Then hops, I suppose, are climbers?

MOTHER.

Yes; and the poles are used to encourage their growth, by giving support to the young branches. In countries where wine is made, entire fields are planted with vines, which are supported on poles, just like the hops that you have seen in Kent and Surrey. I am glad that you have asked these questions; and whenever I mention any thing that you do not quite understand, you must not hesitate to say so. And now, while I recollect it, I will tell you the distinctions between the terms Tree, Shrub, and Herb, which are frequently employed by botanists.

Trees are those plants that bear flowers for several years in succession, and which, after sending up a lofty trunk, are divided at the top into many branches.

A Shrub is like a small tree, with a woody stem, which lasts many years also, but begins to be divided into branches near the ground.

Herbs, or Herbaceous plants, have soft, not woody stems. If they bear leaves and seeds within one year and then die, they are called Annuals; when they bear leaves in the first year, and flowers in the second, and then die, they are Biennials; and if they live and flower for more years than two, they are called Perennials.

The Oak, and Horse-Chesnut, are trees; Myrtle and Privet, shrubs; Parsley and Mint, herbs.

Climate and cultivation have great effect upon the growth of all plants, so that the shrubs of cold countries attain, in warmer climates, the size of trees; and in a few instances, even herbaceous plants become as large as the trees in our orchards. On the contrary, the trees of a warm or temperate climate dwindle into shrubs in a cold one. The colours, too, of the tropical flowers, particularly those of Asia, are much richer and more variegated than those of cold countries, which are principally white and blue.

EDWARD.

What is the meaning of Tropical?

MOTHER.

It is a term used in geography, that you will find explained in your books on that subject: but I intended by Tropical plants, only to signify those that grow in the warmest climates of the world. The space that lies between what are called the Tropics, is more directly under the influence of the sun, and is much warmer than any other part of the globe.

But I must not omit the Lil'ium, a genus which belongs to the Sixth Class, and is one of the most important in a very numerous tribe known under the general name of Lilies.

The flowers of this genus are very beautiful, being shaped like a bell, and composed of six petals, generally of the most brilliant colours. The roots are round and fleshy Bulbs: — a sort of root of which there are several different kinds; and of which the Crocus and Snow-drop afford good examples. (See Plates 4 and 7.) In the tulip, the bulbous root is solid, hard, and smooth: in the lily it is scaly, something like the skin of a fish, or the cup of a thistle; and in the onion, it is coated, which means composed of layers one over another.

The bulbous root of the Kamschatka lily, Lil'ium

Camschatcen'se, called by the natives Saranne, forms a principal part of the food of the inhabitants of that country. Providentially this plant is very abundant in Kamschatka; all the grounds there blooming with its flowers during the season. At the periods when fish is scarce, the Saranne is plentiful, and when there is a dearth of this food the rivers supply provision. The roots are gathered by the women, dried in the sun, and laid up for use. After being baked they are ground to powder, which serves as the flour that the best Kamschatkan bread is made of; and they are also sometimes eaten like potatoes.

But it is not to the labour of the women alone that the Kamschatkans are indebted for a stock of these roots: a species of mouse saves them a great deal of trouble in procuring it. The Saranne forms part of the winter-provisions of that little animal, which not only gathers them in the proper season and lays them up in its magazines, but has the foresight to bring them out to dry in sunny weather to prevent their decaying. The natives search for these hoards, but always take care to leave a part for the mice, to save those useful little creatures from perishing for want of food.

CONVERSATION THE NINTH.

CLASS 7. HEPTANDRIA. — TRIENTALIS. — HORSE-CHESNUT TREE. — CLASS 8. OCTANDRIA. — HEATHS. — DAPHNE MEZEREUM, COMMON MEZEREON, EXAMINED. — MAPLE. — NUT-TREE. — WALNUT. — POPLAR. — CORK-TREE. — OAK; ITS VARIOUS USES. — CLASS 9. ENNEANDRIA. — BUTOMUS UMBELLATUS, FLOWERING RUSH, EXAMINED. — LAUREL-TREE. — CINNAMON. — CAMPHOR. — RHUBARB.

MOTHER.

We are now come to the least numerous of all the classes, the Seventh, Heptandria, of which there is but one genus native in England, and of that there is only one species known, the chickweed winter-green, Trienta'lis Europæ'a. It grows in woods and on turfy heaths in the northern counties, but you are not likely to meet with it in our own neighbourhood.

The Horse-chesnut, Æs'culus hippocas'tanum, in the first order of the class Heptandria, is a native of the northern parts of Asia, from whence it was introduced into Europe, about the year 1500. There are several trees of it in our plantations, and you know how beautiful the flowers are in the month of May. The tree affords a fine shade while the leaves remain upon it, but as they begin to fall off in July, it soon loses its beauty. Deer are particularly fond of the nuts; which in Turkey are ground and mixed with the horses' food.

EDWARD.

Is the wood of the Horse-chesnut made any use of?

MOTHER.

None, that I know of, except for water-pipes under-ground; but I have heard that its bark is sometimes used in medicine.

The eighth class, OCTANDRIA, contains a very numerous and beautiful genus, that of the Heaths, Eri'ca, which is confined entirely to Europe and the southern parts of Africa. The country about the Cape of Good Hope is, of all others, the most abundant in them; and it is said that the Cape alone produces more than two hundred and fifty species. Our native heaths, of which there are five species, though inferior to the foreign ones, are very beautiful. The most common, Eulga'ris, is very useful to the poor inhabitants of the north of

Scotland, who make beds, and thatch the roofs of their cottages with it. In England and Ireland brooms are made of its branches; and in the island of Islay, (one of the Western Isles,) ale is sometimes made of the young tops, with the addition of a little malt. The bee extracts a great deal of honey from the flowers of heath.

Here is a drawing of the common Mezereon [see PLATE 8.] a plant in the order Monogynia of this class; which you must be contented with for this year, as the plant itself flowers in February and March, and is now out of blow.

EDWARD.

Then will you read a description of it, while I look at the drawing; and next spring we can try to find some real mezereon in the hedges?

MOTHER.

It is not a very common plant, and I do not think you will find it growing wild in this part of the country; but that in our garden is of the same species, and will do as well for examination. The generic name is Daphne, and the characters of the genus are these: — It has no calyx; the blossom is of one petal, shaped like a funnel; the tube of the blossom is longer than the border, which last has four flat divisions, ending in points. There are eight stamens, growing on the inside of the tube

Flower opened

Daphne Mezereum _ *Common Mezereon.*

Class VIII ***OCTANDRIA*** _ **Order** ***MONOGYNIA.***

Milton sc

Published April [illegible] by Longman & Co

in two rows, four of them below the other four, but placed alternately. The germen is egg-shaped, and contained within the blossom; the style very short. The seed-vessel is a pulpy round berry, which contains a single seed.

Withering mentions three native species; and the character which distinguishes the Meze′reum from the others consists in the flowers being sessile, or sitting close, without any flower-stalks, and growing upon the sides of the stem, generally three together. The leaves, which are spear-shaped, grow from the ends of the branches, and fall off in the autumn. The berries are red, and Linnæus says that they are so poisonous, that six of them will kill a wolf.

EDWARD.

Is the Mezereon a shrub or a tree?

MOTHER.

It is only a shrub, as you may perceive from its throwing out branches so near the ground.

There is another species of Daphne, the Lagetto, called the Lace bark tree, from the resemblance of its inner bark to net-work or lace. This bark is very beautiful, and consists of several layers that may be easily pulled out into a fine white silky web, three or four feet wide, like lace or gauze, which has often been used for ladies' dresses: and Swartz, a celebrated botanist, says that it may be washed without injury. King Charles the Second is said to have had a cravat made of this web, presented to him by the governor of Jamaica; of which island and of Hispaniola, it is a native.

The common Maple-tree, Acer campes'tre, and the Sycamore, or Plane Tree, Acer pseudo-plat'anus, are placed by Withering * in the same class and order as the Mezereon, and both are natives of England. The wood of the first species is much used by musical instrument makers, on account of its lightness; and that of the Sycamore is one of the best that can be employed for turning; — it was in universal use for trenchers before the introduction of earthen-ware. The Sugar Maple, Acer sacchari'num, grows in great abundance in Pensylvania, where the inhabitants make sugar in large quantities from the juice or sap, which they obtain by piercing the stem of the tree in spring. This sugar is made pretty much in the same manner as that procured from the sugar-cane, of which you read an account a few evenings ago.

The Whortle-berry or Bilberry, Vaccin'ium Myrtil'lus, and Cranberry, Vaccin'ium Oxycoc'cus, are in the first order of this class, and grow plentifully in Scotland and some parts of England.

* In the 23d class, Polygamia, and order Monoecia of Linnæus.

The whortle-berries are the principal food of the moor-game in Scotland; and cranberries are so much liked for making tarts, that they are brought to London from the northern counties, and even imported from Russia; as are also the berries of another species of Vacci'nium, nearly resembling the European, but with larger fruit, from North America.

The Hasel-nut tree, Cor'ylus avella'na, in the order Digynia of this class, according to Withering *, grows very commonly in our woods, and its timber is used for several different purposes. I need not describe the nuts to you, for you saw them yesterday at dinner. Squirrels live almost entirely upon them, and the leaves of the trees are eaten by horses.

EDWARD.

What tree is it that produces walnuts?

MOTHER.

The Ju'glans re'gia, which was originally brought from Persia, but now grows commonly in this country. The genus Ju'glans is in the class Monoecia of Linnæus. The tree grows to the height of fifty feet, and bears clusters of large green fruit, inclosing furrowed nuts, which ripen in September and October: the young fruit is pickled, and when ripe, the kernels are eaten. It is from these

* Class 21. Monoecia, order Polyandria, of Linnæus.

nuts that what is called nut-oil is obtained, but the hazel-nut also affords a kind of oil which is used by painters. The wood of the walnut-tree takes a fine polish; but is too brittle to be used where great strength is necessary.

I had almost forgotten to tell you, that the Poplar, of which there are three or four native species, belongs, according to Withering, to the order Monogynia, of the eighth class.* The bark of the Aspin-tree, or trembling poplar, Pop'ulus trem'ula, which is one of them, is the principal food of beavers: and Linnæus says, that it serves as fodder for cows, goats, and sheep in West Bothnia (a part of Sweden), being cut into very small pieces in autumn, and laid up to dry till the following spring, when it is used instead of hay, which is very scarce there at that season.

The bark of the Black poplar, Pop'ulus ni'gra, is so light, that it is sometimes employed instead of cork, to support the nets of fishermen in the water.

EDWARD.

But what is real cork?

MOTHER.

It is the outer bark of a species of oak, Quercus su'ber, (of a genus placed by Withering in the

* Class and order Dioecia Octandria of Linnæus.

class Octandria*,) which grows in the south of Europe and the north of Africa.

The cork tree does not begin to be productive until it is fifteen years old, and even then the bark is only fit for fuel, nor does it arrive at perfection until about the twenty-third year; but from that period it continues, for about an hundred and fifty years, to yield good cork every tenth year. The season for stripping off the cork is in July and August, and great care is taken not to wound the inner bark, which in time becomes good cork also. The best sort comes from Spain and Portugal; and is imported in great quantities into England, where it is cut into corks for bottles, and applied to many other purposes. The Spaniards cover the walls of their houses with cork like wainscotting, which not only makes them very warm, but very dry; and the peasantry in Spain lay broad planks of it at their bed-sides, as we do carpets; they also burn it, to make what is called by painters Spanish black. The Egyptians formerly made coffins of cork lined with resin, which preserved their dead bodies for a long time.

Two species of Quercus or Oak-tree grow naturally in England, one of which, the Quercus ro'bur, is particularly valuable; it is indeed the most important of our native trees. It is remark-

* Monoecia Polyandria, of Linnæus.

ably long lived, and attains a great size, the full-grown trees sometimes measuring from fifty to sixty feet round. The wood is hard and tough, takes a good polish, and, when well manufactured, has a very handsome appearance. The roofs and frame-work of almost all our ancient buildings that are the best preserved, are formed of this timber, and it is now always employed where strength and durability are required. The crooked branches of the oak are of peculiar value in building ships, and there are extensive forests in England belonging to the King, which are reserved entirely for that purpose. Oak saw-dust is one of the principal vegetable ingredients used in dying the different shades of brown and drab colour. The bark of the tree is universally used for tanning leather; and the acorns or fruit, which enclose the seed, for fattening deer and pigs.

Those light spongy bodies, about the size of walnuts, called oak-apples, which you have often seen, are excrescences that grow from the leaves and other tender parts of this tree, when wounded by insects in depositing their eggs: they are called also galls, and there are several different kinds occasioned by different insects. Some of them are very useful in dying black, and the common gall is an essential ingredient in the ink that we write with.

The plants of the ninth class, ENNEANDRIA, are so few in number, that I think we can go through them to-day; and I dare say it will give you pleasure to examine this one that I have just procured for you. [See PLATE 9.]

EDWARD.

How beautiful it is! I long to find out its name.

MOTHER.

That you can easily do; for there are but three native genera in this class, according to Withering, and only one in the arrangement of Linnæus. Here, take the plant in your hand, while I read what Withering says about the genera.

The first genus described, Mercuria'lis *, is in the order Digynia; it has no blossom, and the flowers with stamens are on different plants from those with pistils: we need not read any farther about it, for your plant, having six pistils, is in the order Hexagynia; and it has a blossom with stamens and pistils in each flower.

In the second genus, Bu'tomus, the calyx, which is called an Involucrum, is composed of three leaves.

EDWARD.

But these flowers have no calyx.

MOTHER.

It is true that each flower has not a separate calyx; but if you look at the top of the stem, from

* In the class and order Monoecia Enneandria, of Linnæus.

which the flower-stalks grow, something in the manner of an umbelliferous plant, you will perceive three sharp-pointed brownish leaves, that form a sort of general calyx to the umbel or set of flowers: this is called an Involucrum. The blossom is round, hollowed out like a bowl, and composed of six petals; three of them smaller than the rest, and standing alternately on the outside between the others. There are nine stamens, the filaments awl-shaped, and the anthers composed of two flat pieces laid close together; and six pistils, each consisting of a germen, that gradually passes into a style, with a summit slightly notched.

In the next genus of Withering, Hydrocha'ris *, the stamens and pistils are in the flowers of different plants; so that Bu'tomus must be our genus, of which there is but one species known, called umbella'tus, from the resemblance of its sets of flowers to an umbel. The English name is Flowering Rush, and it grows on the margins of lakes and slow-running rivers.

EDWARD.

I wish we could always have real plants to examine; it is so much more easy to remember them than the drawings.

MOTHER.

So do I, my dear; and I hope we shall succeed in finding some in the classes that we have still to

* Class and order Dioecia Enneandria, of Linnæus.

Bútomus umbellátus _ *Flowering Rush.*

Class IX *ENNEANDRIA* _ Order *HEXAGYNIA.*

Milton sc.

Published April 2.1817 by Longman & C°.

go through; but it is not possible to obtain them all at the same period of the year.

The genus Laurus, or laurel, is in the order Monogynia, of the Ninth class; but none of the species grow wild in England.

The sweet Bay-tree, Laurus nob'ilis, is a native of Italy, and is said to be the true laurel of the ancients, with which they crowned their generals when they gained victories. It is a fine aromatic evergreen, and grows to the height of thirty feet.

The Cinnamon-tree, Laurus cinnamo'mum, is a native of Ceylon. The whole plant is covered with a bark, at first green, and afterwards red: when the tree is three or four years old, this bark is peeled off, cut into narrow slips, and dried in the sun, when it curls up into quills or flakes, which are the cinnamon we see in the shops. The fruit is shaped like an acorn, but is not so large. When the seeds are boiled in water, they yield an oil, that hardens into a white substance, which has a delightful smell, and at Ceylon, was made into candles, for the use of the king only.

The Camphor-tree, Laurus cam'phora, so called from its affording the substance called camphor, is a species that grows in Japan, and is there a large and valuable timber-tree. It is used in the best buildings, as well as for the masts of ships.

Rhubarb, Rhe'um, is an herbaceous plant in the order Trigynia of the Ninth class. The common sort, Rhe'um Rhapon'ticum, is a native of Turkey-in-Asia, but is frequently planted in our gardens; and we use the young leaf-stalks in spring for tarts. The Chinese rhubarb, Rhe'um palma'tum, and a species that grows in Tartary, Rhe'um compactum, have thick, fleshy, yellow roots, which are much used in medicine.

We shall leave the Tenth class for to-morrow; as I think you have heard quite enough for the present.

CONVERSATION THE TENTH.

CLASS 10. DECANDRIA. — STRAWBERRY TREE. — SAXIFRAGE. — PINK. — DOUBLE AND SINGLE FLOWERS. — CARNATION. — AGROSTEMMA GITHAGO, CORN-COCKLE, EXAMINED. — WOOD SORREL. — LIGNUM VITÆ TREE. — LOGWOOD. — BRAZIL-WOOD. — MAHOGANY TREE.

MOTHER.

THE common Strawberry-tree, Ar'butus une'do, is one of the species most remarkable for beauty amongst the native plants of the class Decandria. It belongs to the order Monogynia, and grows wild in Ireland, Italy, and Spain. The time of its flowering is November or December, but the fruit does not ripen till the following winter; and it is singular to see, at that season, a tree in the open ground covered with both flowers and fruit; for when the fruit is ripe, and still remaining on the tree, the flowers for the succeeding crop are in full bloom.

EDWARD.

The berries look like red strawberries: I have tasted some of them in the shrubbery, but they were not very good.

MOTHER.

They are insipid; but they are sometimes eaten by the country-people in the south of Ireland, where this tree grows abundantly, and in great perfection, especially among the rocks at the Lakes of Killarney.

The black berried strawberry-tree, Ar'butus alpi'na, which grows on mountains in Scotland, flowers in June and July, and bears a fruit that resembles black currants, both in shape and flavour.

The second order, Digynia, of this class, contains a genus Saxif'raga, or Saxifrage, of which there are several native species. The London-pride, Saxif'raga umbro'sa, is one of them; and although this plant is so common in all our gardens, its natural situation is on high mountains.

The beautiful genus of Pinks, Dian'thus, which includes all the varieties of carnations and sweet-williams, is also in this order; and there are five or six native species of it. The fine double carnations, that are so much admired, are only varieties of the common pink, Dian'thus caryophyl'lus, which, in its wild state bears single flowers.

EDWARD.

What are double flowers?

MOTHER.

All flowers, which have a greater number of petals than usual, are commonly called double; but, strictly speaking, they should be called also treble, quadruple, and so on, according to the number of rows of the petals. Great richness of soil, and high cultivation, have such an effect upon plants, that they grow very luxuriantly; and the stamens, in some kinds, are converted into petals. When all the stamens are changed in this way, the flower is called full, and can no longer produce seeds; and in order to bring back the plant to its natural state, we ought to put it into a poorer soil, or in other words, to give it less food, or not of so rich a quality. Flowers with many petals often become full; but, those of one petal are more disposed to be changed into double or treble, &c. which botanists call being multiplied. In either state, they are generally thought to be more beautiful, and are very much valued by gardeners; but a botanist considers every thing as a deformity that is not natural to a plant in its uncultivated state. If I wished to examine a species of Dianthus, I should choose a wild specimen with a single flower.

EDWARD.

But don't you like the double carnations a great deal better than the single pinks and sweet-williams?

MOTHER.

I certainly do admire the wonderful variety and beauty of their colours. —Can you read these lines?

EDWARD.

Where is the labour of the loom
Can vie with the Carnation's bloom?
He who can thus adorn a flower,
That's doom'd to perish in an hour,
Forbids his creatures to despair
His universal love to share.

MOTHER.

Here is a plant that I brought in this morning to examine. [See PLATE 10.] Can you tell me its class and order?

EDWARD.

It must be in the tenth class, Decandria, and the order Pentagynia; for it has ten stamens, and five pistils.

MOTHER.

Very well; now compare it with this description: —Calyx, a cup of one leaf, of a texture something like that of leather, with five sharp divisions; blossom composed of five petals; the lower parts of the

Agrostemma Githágo . *Corn Cockle.*

Class X. *DECANDRIA*. Order *PENTAGYNIA*.

Milton sc

Published April 2, 1817 by Longman & C°.

petals, which are called claws, as long as the tube of the cup; border of the blossom spreading out. The filaments are awl-shaped; and the styles of the pistils thread-shaped, as long as the stamens, with undivided summits. This is the generic character of Agrostem'ma, and you see it answers very well. There is but one species native: the specific character consists in the whole plant being hairy; the cup having ten ribs, with divisions reaching beyond the blossom; and the petals being undivided and without down or hair. The English name is Corn-Cockle, and the botanical one Agrostem'ma Githa'go.

EDWARD.

I think I have seen it in corn-fields.

MOTHER.

I dare say you have, for it grows in abundance amongst corn; and is a troublesome weed.

The pretty little Wood Sorrel, Ox'alis acetosel'la, is in the same order. The leaves of this plant, which are shaped like those of the trefoil, close up on the approach of rain; and when it is dry, they open again, and hang down: they are very acid, like those of the common sorrel, Ru'mex aceto'sa, and a salt is prepared from them, which is sold in the shops under the name of essential salt of lemon.

EDWARD.

Are there any trees in the tenth class?

MOTHER.

I do not know of many, and none of them except the Ar'butus are native; but I will tell you of a few foreign ones that I recollect.

The Lignum vitæ tree, Gui'acum officina'le, in the order Monogynia of this class, is a native of the West-Indies. The wood is so heavy that it sinks in water, and so hard that it breaks the tools which are employed in cutting it down: it is, therefore, seldom used for common purposes; but is of great use to sugar-planters, for making wheels in their sugar-mills, and is frequently made into bowls, mortars, and other utensils.

It is said that the wood, bark, the gum (called gum-guaiacum), the fruit, and even the flowers of this tree, are useful in medicine.

The Logwood-tree, Hæmatox'ylon Campechia'num, which is of the greatest use in dying and in staining wood, is a native of South America. It is very heavy, and is brought to Europe in logs of about a yard long, which are cut and bruised by a mill before they can be used by the dyer.

The Brazil-wood, Cæsalpi'nia Brasilien'sis, which is used for similar purposes, particularly for dying cloth of a beautiful scarlet colour, comes from the

West-Indies. The wood is very hard and dry, of a red colour, and takes a good polish.

The Egyptian Cassia, or Senna-tree, Cassia Senna, which produces the leaves that are used in medicine, is a native of Persia, Syria, and Arabia. The leaves are gathered in those countries, and sent to Alexandria in Egypt, from whence they are brought to Europe.

The Mahogany tree is the last I shall mention in this class. Its botanical name is Swiete'nia Mahog'ani: and it grows in the warmest parts of America, and some of the West-Indian islands. The seeds, which are very light, are often blown into the chinks of rocks, where they take root, and at length produce trees of considerable size: and the wood of those that spring in this manner, from exposed situations, is harder and better than what grows in other places.

Mahogany is found to answer better than any other timber for cabinet makers' work, for it takes a fine polish, and is very durable. It was first brought to England about a hundred years ago, by a West-India captain, as ballast for his ship; and being found too hard to be cut with the common tools used by carpenters, was laid aside as useless; but, afterwards, it is said, the captain's wife being in want of a box to hold her candles, thought that a kind of wood so hard would answer very well for keeping out the mice, and had stronger tools employed to make one. The wood was then found to be so beautiful, that the fame of mahogany became general, and it has ever since been imported in large quantities.

I do not wish to tell you any thing more at present, my dear, as it will be better for you to remember well what you have already heard: and if you attempt to learn too much at one time, you can retain nothing in your memory.

To-morrow morning we will go into the village, and look for some Houseleek, which grows on the roofs of cottages and the tops of old walls; it is the best plant that I can think of for examination in the eleventh class, and there is but one native species. But we must try to find some of it growing in different situations, for a reason that I shall tell you when we examine the plant.

CONVERSATION THE ELEVENTH.

CLASS 11. DODECANDRIA.—SEMPERVIVUM TECTORUM, COMMON HOUSELEEK, EXAMINED.—DEFECTS OF SYSTEMS.—MIGNONETTE.—CHESNUT-TREE.—BEECH.—CLASS 12. ICOSANDRIA.—IMPORTANCE OF THE SITUATION OF THE STAMENS.—ROSA CANINA, DOG-ROSE, EXAMINED.—ROSES.—SWEET-BRIAR.—FRUIT-TREES OF THIS CLASS.—HAWTHORN.—CLOVE-TREE.—MYRTLE.—PEACH, AND ALMOND TREES.

EDWARD.

Are you ready now, mamma, to read a description of the Houseleek?

MOTHER.

Yes, my dear. I wish I could have procured a flower that would show the character of the class Dodecandria, more distinctly: but the number of stamens varies under different circumstances, even in the same species of the genera that are native. The Houseleek, however, is certainly placed in this class by botanists. Can you tell me the order it is in?

EDWARD.

I suppose it is Dodecagynia, for I see twelve pistils, and I think you told me that whenever there were about that number in each flower, the order was called so.

MOTHER.

You are right. The number of the pistils in the genus Sempervi'vum, to which this plant belongs, is commonly twelve; but it often varies. Here then is the description. —[See PLATE 11.] The calyx is a cup, of one piece, with twelve or more sharp divisions; the blossom is longer than the cup, and composed of the same number of sharp petals, each of which is fringed with fine hairs. The number of stamens is in general the same with that of the petals; but frequently, in this species, some of them are imperfect, and of very different appearance from the rest. There are about twelve germens, placed in a circle, which have sharp summits. In our plant, the Sempervi'vum tecto'rum, the leaves grow in thick tufts, and are very fleshy and fringed at the edges with hair.

EDWARD.

Look at this piece that grew upon the wall; it has only eight pistils.

MOTHER.

In the Houseleek you will often find, that the

Sempervivum tectórum _ *Common Houseleek.*

Milton sc.

Class XI. *DODECANDRIA* _ Order *DODECAGYNIA.*

Published April 1.1817 by Longman & Co.

number of all the parts of the flower, especially the pistils, varies according to the richness of the soil in which the plant has grown; and it was for this reason that I wished to bring home specimens from different situations. The branch that we have just examined was from the thatched roof of the cottage, where I suppose the soil was richer than on the top of the wall.

EDWARD.

I am afraid that I should not have been able to find out the name of this plant, if you had not told me.

MOTHER.

It is, certainly, unsatisfactory to examine the plants that are placed in this class, because the character itself is imperfect. You must always recollect, that every botanical arrangement (or system, as it is called) must be defective, because the knowledge of plants, even with the best botanists, is very far from being complete. The method of Linnæus is upon the whole the best, but it has some faults; and this is one of its most imperfect parts. The eleventh class is formed merely for convenience, and has no foundation in nature; whereas the grasses, and some other tribes of plants that I have told you of, besides having a natural character that distinguishes them, are very regular in the number and situation of the different parts, upon which the classes and orders are founded.

The genus Rese'da, of which the Mignonette is a species, belongs also to the class Dodecandria; and Linnæus himself says, that there is scarcely any genus, whose character it is more difficult to determine; the number and shape of the parts of the flower varying considerably in different species. There are two of these native in England, the Rese'da lu'tea, or wild Reseda, and the Lute'ola, Dyer's-weed. The latter plant is made great use of in the woollen manufactories for dying yellow, and it gives the colour also to the yellow paint called Dutch pink: It flowers in July; and Linnæus has observed that the spike of flowers follows the course of the sun, turning towards the East at sunrise, towards the West as the sun declines, and at midnight pointing to the North.

The garden Mignonette, Rese'da odora'ta, is a native of Egypt; and these three species are all annual. Do you recollect what that word means?

EDWARD.

An annual is a plant that bears leaves and flowers in one year, and then dies.

MOTHER.

Very well. Many plants that are annual in warmer climates, become biennial, or live for two years with us; because the heat of this country is not sufficient to bring them to perfection in one year, and the seeds do not ripen till the second summer: and some that in warm countries are perennial, (which means lasting many years,) become annual with us, the root being killed by our severe winters.

But we must return to the eleventh class, and finish it, that we may go on to the twelfth, which is very extensive, and contains several plants that you will be pleased to hear of.

The Chesnut tree, Fa'gus casta'nea, which, according to Withering, is in the order Trigynia, of the class Dodecandria *, is one of the finest of our native trees, and is remarkably long-lived. In Gloucestershire there is one, which is proved to have stood there ever since the year 1150, and was even then so remarkable, as to be called the great Chesnut of Tortworth: it measures fifty-two feet round, and still continues to bear fruit, though probably not less than a thousand years old. The largest chesnut-trees that are known in the world grow upon Mount Ætna in Sicily. The wood is very valuable, and the nuts form a great part of the food of the common people in the south of Europe.

The common Beech, Fa'gus sylvat'ica, is also a native of England. This tree retains its old

* In the class and order Monoecia Polyandria, of Linneus.

leaves through the winter; and they are often gathered in the autumn by the poor people, for the purpose of making mattrasses, which are much better and more durable than those of straw or chaff. The wood soon decays when exposed to the weather; but lasts a long time under water, and is of the greatest value for making carpenters' tools. The nuts, when dried and ground, are said to make a tolerable sort of bread, but they cause giddiness, if eaten raw: The poor people of Silesia use an oil procured from them, instead of butter.

Now, Edward, tell me if you recollect how the twelfth class, ICOSANDRIA, is distinguished from the others?

EDWARD.

I believe there are more than twenty stamens in each flower; and if the petals are pulled off, the stamens remain on the receptacle.

MOTHER.

Bring your little drawing of the classes, and see, yourself, whether you are right. [See PLATE 2.]

EDWARD.

Oh, I have made a great mistake! — It is in the thirteenth class, Polyandria, that the stamens grow upon the receptacle. In Icosandria they are fastened to the sides of the calyx.

MOTHER.

Here are two plants; a Dog-rose and a Butter-cup; tell me to what class each of them belongs?

EDWARD.

I have pulled off the calyx of both flowers, and I find that the rose is in the class Icosandria, and the butter-cup in Polyandria; for all the stamens of the Rose came off along with the calyx, but in the butter-cup they remain on the receptacle.

MOTHER.

Exactly so. This character of the class Icosandria is very important; as it indicates, almost infallibly, that the pulpy fruit which accompanies it, is wholesome. No traveller in an unknown wilderness need be afraid to eat the fruit of any plant whose stamens grow upon the calyx; but the other parts should be carefully avoided, for in some species they are poisonous.*

The plant that we shall examine to-day, is a rose, which belongs to the genus Rosa, in the order Polygynia; and as there are several native species, I will at once tell you that this is the common dog-rose, Rosa cani'na. [See PLATE 12.] The cup in this genus is of one leaf; with five divisions in its border, which are narrow and sharp

* Smith's Introduction to Botany, 3d edition, pp. 298, 324.

pointed. The blossom has five heart-shaped petals, as long as the cup, and fixed to its neck. You recollect, that in this class, the precise number of the stamens is not material; but there are more than twenty. The filaments are short, and fixed to the sides of the calyx. There is no seed-vessel; but the cup itself swells into a berry, which is coloured (generally bright red) when ripe, and contains numerous oblong seeds rough with stiff hair. It is this cup which forms the principal distinction of the genus Rosa: in shape it is something like a boy's top, bulging below and drawn in at the neck or upper part, as if confined by a string; and it opens at top to let out the ripe seeds.

The species Cani'na is distinguished from the others, by having oblong fruit, the stalks that bear the flowers smooth, and those that support the leaves prickly: and two crooked prickles between the knots of the stem, placed alternately on opposite sides. Two of the divisions of the calyx have teeth on both edges; two have none; and the fifth has teeth on one edge only.

EDWARD.

How pretty the dog-roses are! I often wish to bring some home; but the thorns are so sharp, that I can hardly pull them in the hedges.

Rósa canína _ *Common Dog Rose.*

Class XII *ICOSANDRIA* _ _ Order *POLYGYNIA*.

Milton

MOTHER.

They are always acompanied by thorns, and these lines were written to reconcile us to them—

Why does the painful thorn presume
To spoil the rose's soft perfume?—
It was by Providence intended,
Our pains and pleasures should be blended;
We smile to-day, to-morrow mourn,
Nor find a rose without a thorn.

The sweet-briar is another species of rose, Rosa rubigino'sa, which is common in England: its flowers sometimes grow double, and as well as the leaves have a very delightful scent. Roses are the favourite plants in all countries where they are found; but it is remarkable that none have ever been met with in the southern hemisphere.

There is another genus in this class, and of the same order, the bramble, Ru'bus, that in some respects resembles the rose tribe. Most of the species grow in cool climates or mountainous situations, and are valuable for their fruit., which is wholesome and agreeable. The berry is composed of a number of juicy grains, in general so attached to each other that they cannot be separated without tearing, which are collected into a head, that is hollow underneath, and placed upon a spongy conical receptacle.

The wild raspberry, Ru'bus idæ'us, is plentiful

in the north of England, Scotland, and Wales, and though smaller than what is cultivated in gardens, (which is a variety of the same species,) the fruit has a much sweeter flavour. The fresh leaves are the favourite food of kids. The blackberry, which is so common in all our hedges, is the Ru'bus frutico'sus.

The cloud-berry, Ru'bus chamæmo'rus, has its English name from growing on the tops of very high mountains, which are often covered by clouds. It grows plentifully in the north of England and Scotland, and in many parts of the north of Europe. The Norwegians pack up the berries in wooden vessels, and send them to Stockholm, where they are sold for desserts; and the Laplanders bury them under the snow to preserve them from one year to another.

The plum, Pru'nus; the medlar, Mes'pilus; and the pear and apple tree, Py'rus, belong also to this class, and are all found wild in England.

The cherry, plum, and apricot are different species of the genus Pru'nus, and though the fruit is so good, the leaves of several of the species are poisonous; those of one of them, Pru'nus Laurocer'asus, or Laurel cherry, remarkably so.

The apricot has its specific name of Armeni'aca, from having been originally a native of Armenia; it was first brought to this country about two hundred and fifty years ago.

All the varieties of pears and apples belong to two species only of Py'rus. The wood of the pear-tree, Py'rus commu'nis, is light and smooth, and is much used for making carved work: and the picture-frames, that are so common, are also made of it, stained black. The juice of the fruit fermented, is called perry; which is made in large quantities in England, particularly in Worcestershire and Herefordshire.

The wild apple, or crab-tree, Py'rus ma'lus, though so harsh and disagreeable, is the original from which all our varieties of apples have been produced. The tree lives a long time; and the wood is much used by millwrights. The juice of the wild fruit, which is extremely sour, is called verjuice, but that of the cultivated kinds, when fermented, makes cyder.

The strawberry, Fraga'ria, is another valuable genus of this class, and is native in England.—

EDWARD.

Are the large strawberries in our garden of the same genus as the little ones, that we find in the woods?

MOTHER.

They are; and even the species is the same, Fraga'ria vesca; but the fruit is enlarged to the size that you see in the garden by cultivation and richness of soil; which, you remember, I told you had a great effect upon almost all plants.

The hawthorn, Cratæ'gus Oxyacan'thus, which grows in almost every hedge, and the mountain-ash, Sorbus aucupa'ria, that is so ornamental in shrubberies, are in the orders Digynia and Trigynia, of the class Icosandria.

Among the foreign genera of this class, the clove-tree, the myrtle, and the peach and almond trees, are remarkable.

The clove-tree, Euge'nia caryophylla'ta, belongs to the order Monogynia, and is a native of the Molucca islands. Its general appearance resembles that of a laurel. The flowers, which are produced at the ends of the branches in great quantities, are first white, then green, and at last red and hard, in which state they are the cloves. The season for gathering this spice, is from October to February, when large cloths are spread under the trees to receive the flowers, which are beaten off the boughs with long reeds: As they dry they become yellow; and when gathered for some time, they are of a deep brown colour, such as we see.

The common myrtle, the pretty evergreen shrub, that is to be found in every green-house, is the species Commu'nis, of the genus Myrtus; and is a native of Asia, Africa, and the southern parts of Europe. Lord Anson mentions, in his voyage round the world, that the largest trees that could be procured for timber on the island of Juan Fernandez, and from which he obtained beams of forty feet in length, were of this genus.

The peach-tree, Amyg'dalus Per'sica, of which there are two varieties, the Peach with downy, and the Nectarine with smooth fruit, is in the first order of this class. Its native country is not known, but it is supposed to have come originally from Persia. The almond-tree, another species, Amyg'dalus commu'nis, is a native of Barbary.

CONVERSATION THE TWELFTH.

CLASS 13. POLYANDRIA. — PAPAVER RHÆAS, COMMON POPPY, EXAMINED. — SEEDS. — OPIUM. — TEA-TREE. — CAPER-BUSH. — WATER-LILY. — TULIP TREE. — ANOTTA. — STORY OF AN INDIAN WOMAN.

EDWARD.

I HAVE brought in some beautiful poppies from the corn-fields; and I am sure they are in the thirteenth class, Polyandria, for all the stamens are fixed to the receptacle, and there are more than twenty of them. Will you read the description of the poppy for me?

MOTHER.

I will, my dear, with pleasure. It gives me great satisfaction to find that you begin to distinguish the classes by yourself. But we must go on regularly: — Is there nothing else to be determined before we come to the genus?

EDWARD.

Oh, yes! — the order. Well, there is only one pistil, so it is Monogynia.

MOTHER.

Very well. The genera of this order are, for convenience, divided into three sets; consisting of plants which have flowers with four petals, or with five, or a greater number. This plant has but four; and in that division there are only three genera, to one of which of course the poppy belongs.

The seed-vessel of the first genus, Chelido'nium, is a long pod, something like that of the wall-flower. [See Plate 1.] Is that the case in your plant? — Look at the largest of the seed-vessels, and tell me.

EDWARD.

No, mamma; this has a round smooth seed-vessel, with a little thing like a coach-wheel on the top.

MOTHER.

Then it is not Chelido'nium. In the next genus that has four petals, Actæ'a, the seed-vessel is a berry, consisting of a pulpy substance, with the seeds dispersed through it, like a currant or gooseberry, and quite unlike this one. Our plant then must be a Papa'ver; and we will now try whether your flower agrees with the full description of that genus.

The cup consists of two egg-shaped leaves,—

EDWARD.

But these flowers have no cup.

MOTHER.

You must look at some of them that are not fully blown [See PLATE 13.]; for the calyx falls off as soon as the blossom opens.

The cup consists of two egg-shaped leaves, notched at the ends. The blossom is composed of four round flat petals, large and spreading out, and narrowest at the end next to the receptacle. The filaments are numerous, like hair, and much shorter than the blossom; and the anthers are oblong and flattened. The germen of the pistil is large, and in general, nearly round like a globe; but in some of the species it is oblong, as in this instance; there is no style; and the summit is shaped like a target, (or something like a saucer turned upside down,) flat, and divided into rays like the spokes of a wheel. The seed-vessel is called a capsule, and is of one cell, divided half-way through by little partitions that run from top to bottom; and the large flat summit forms a sort of crown upon the top of the seed-vessel, which, when the seeds are ripe, opens in several places close under the crown, to let them out. The seeds are round and numerous.

PLATE 13

Papáver Rhœas _ *Common Red Poppy*.

Class XIII. *POLYANDRIA* _ Order *MONOGYNIA*.

Milton sc.

Published April 2. 1817, by Longman & Co.

EDWARD.

What is a cell?

MOTHER.

It is a hollow space in the seed-vessel, for holding the seeds. A capsule is composed either of one such hollow, or of several; and these cells are sometimes provided with little partitions, to which the seeds are fixed until they are quite ripe and fit for sowing. Can you find the seeds of your poppy?

EDWARD.

Yes; but they are very small. Would every one of these little things grow into a plant, if I was to put them into the ground?

MOTHER.

It is probable that a good many of them would be destroyed by damp, or eaten by insects; which is perhaps one of the reasons why they are so numerous. More than thirty thousand seeds have been found in a single head of poppy; and in some other plants the number is still more surprising. The tobacco, Nicotia'na Tab'acum, of a genus in the class Pentandria, has been known to produce, on one plant, three hundred and sixty thousand seeds.

EDWARD.

Shall we try now to find out what species of poppy this is?

MOTHER.

There are six or seven native species of Papa'ver; two of which, Du'bium and Rhœ'as, resemble each other in their general appearance, and are equally common. As yours is one of these, I will read the characters of both, and you may decide for yourself.

In the species Du'bium, the capsules are oblong, (that is, of an oval shape,) and smooth; the stem bears several flowers; and the stalks are covered with a bristly sort of hair, which lies close down upon them.

In the other species, the capsules are smooth, and shaped like an urn, broader at the top than at the bottom; the stem is hairy, and bears several flowers; and the hair on the fruit-stalks spreads or stands out, instead of lying close down.

EDWARD.

I did not know that poppies had any fruit, but you talk of their fruit-stalks. What are they?

MOTHER.

In all plants, the part that contains the seeds is called the fruit, whether it is fit to be eaten or not; and the fruit-stalks are those which support this part. Now, can you tell me, which of the descriptions that I have just read suits your poppy?

EDWARD.

I think it is the last, because the seed-vessel is broader at the top than at the bottom, and the hairs stand out from the fruit-stalks.

MOTHER.

Very right; our plant is of the last species that I have mentioned, Papa'ver Rhœ'as, the common red poppy; and it is one of the most troublesome weeds the farmer meets with amongst his corn, for it is more difficult to destroy than any other. The seeds will lie a great length of time without shooting, in unploughed land; but as soon as the corn begins to grow, they spring up.

The opium, that is so much used in medicine, is the juice obtained from the unripe seed-vessels of another species of Papa'ver, the somnif'erum, or white poppy. In many parts of Asia Minor, the inhabitants chew a great deal of opium, as the sailors and common people chew tobacco in England; and whole fields are sown with the seeds of this plant, just as ours are with corn. When the heads are nearly ripe, they are wounded on one side with a sharp instrument, and a white liquor flows out, which the heat of the sun hardens upon them; this is the opium: it is collected the next day, when fresh wounds are made on the opposite side of the seed-vessel; but what comes from the first wound is greatly superior to that obtained from the second.

After the opium is collected, it is moistened with a small quantity of water or honey, and worked upon a board until it becomes of the consistence of pitch, when it is formed into cakes or rolls for sale.

There is another plant, called yellow-horned poppy, which is in the same order of this class, but of a different genus, Chelido'nium Glau'cium. It is found in many parts of England near the sea; and has its English name from the great length of the pods, which may be compared to horns. It is a very poisonous plant, as most of those are which belong to the class Polyandria.

EDWARD.

Then, mamma, are there no fruits in this class fit to eat?

MOTHER.

There are a few; but none of them are natives of this country. But there is one tree belonging to it, which is very remarkable, and in several parts of the world, as well as in England, is considered as almost a necessary of life, though it does not produce an eatable fruit. The Tea-tree, The'a, (Polyandria Monogynia), is a native of China, Japan, and Tonquin, and has never been found growing wild in any other country. It attains the height of ten or twelve feet, and is an evergreen: the leaves, which are the only valuable part, are about an inch and a half long, and resemble those of sweet-briar. The flowers are something like the wild white rose; and the seeds are round, blackish, and about the size of a large pea. Linnæus says, that there are two species of this plant, the Bohe'a, or black, and the Vir'idis, or green tea. The green, which has much longer leaves than the black, is a more hardy plant, and, with very little protection, bears the severity of our winters.

As tea is a most important article of commerce to the Chinese, they bestow the greatest possible care upon its cultivation. It is propagated by seeds, which are put into holes about five inches deep, at regular distances from each other; from six to twelve being sown together, as it is supposed that only a small number grow.

When the tree is three years old, the leaves are fit to be gathered; and the men who collect them wear gloves, that the flavour may not be injured. They do not pull them by handfuls, but pick them off one by one, taking great care not to break them: and although this appears to be a very tedious process, each person gathers from ten to fifteen pounds a day.

The fresh leaves are exposed to the steam of boiling water, after which they are put on plates of copper, and held over a fire until they become dry and shrivelled; they are then taken off the plates with a shovel, and spread upon mats; some of the labourers taking a small quantity at a time in their hands, which they roll in one direction; while others are continually employed in stirring those on the mats, in order that they may cool the sooner, and retain their shrivelled appearance: and this process is repeated several times before the tea is fit for use.

The tea leaves are collected at three different seasons. What are first procured, while they are very young, are called imperial tea, which is generally reserved for the court and people of rank, because it is considered as of the finest quality. The last gathering, when the leaves have attained their full growth, is the coarsest tea of all, and is used by the common people.

In China and Japan, tea is sold in every town and on all the public roads, as beer is in England; and is drunk in the same manner by labourers and travellers: it is used without cream or sugar; and in Chinese drawings, the people are seldom represented at work of any kind, without a tea-pot and tea-cup. The people of rank in those countries, take as much pains to procure tea of excellent quality, as the Europeans do to obtain good wine; and they generally keep it a year before they make use of it.

Tea was first brought to Europe from China, by the Dutch merchants, about the year 1641.

The caper-bush, Cap'paris spino'sa (Polyandria Monogynia), grows wild in the Levant. It is as common there as the bramble is with us, growing out of old walls, the chinks of rocks, and amongst rubbish; and is cultivated in the south of Europe, for the sake of the young flower-buds, which are pickled and exported in considerable quantities, and are used at table in England. It is a very beautiful shrub.

But I must return to our native plants, some of which, of this class, are too remarkable to be passed over; particularly the water-lily, which is equal in beauty to almost any foreign flower.

EDWARD.

I have seen the white water-lily, mamma, growing in our ponds. What is its botanical name?

MOTHER.

Nymphæ'a alba, of a genus in the order Monogynia. You must watch it in the evening, when its flowers close and lie down upon the water; at night they sink below the surface, and in the middle of the day, when the weather is bright and hot, they rise some inches above it, and expand. The yellow water-lily, Nymphæ'a lu'tea, is also a very beautiful flower, though much smaller; it grows in the same situations as the white, in ponds and slow running rivers.

The common lime-tree, Til'ia Europæ'a (Polyandria Monogynia), is a native of England. The wood is employed for various purposes; the leaves are dried as winter-food for sheep and goats; and the bark is sometimes made into ropes and fishing-nets. Sugar is prepared in some countries from the sap; and the flowers, which are delightfully fragrant, particularly at night, afford the best honey to bees.

There is a tree in the order Polygynia of this class, a native of North America, which bears a flower very much resembling our garden tulip, and is therefore called the tulip-tree, Lirioden'dron tulipif'era. It grows to the height of seventy or eighty feet, and its wood is used for all sorts of carpenters' work. The flowers, which have six petals, spotted with green, red, white, and yellow, are succeeded by large cones or seed-vessels, but these never ripen in England.

I forgot to mention to you, when we were speaking of the first order of this class, that the dye, called Anotta, is obtained from the berries of a tree belonging to it, called Bixa Orella'na, a native of the East and West Indies. The Mexicans employed the anotta, which affords a bright orange colour, in staining wood and in drawing; and it is used in England to give a deep colour to cheese. The bark makes good ropes for common purposes; and the wood is much used by the American In-

Indians for procuring fire, which they do by rubbing pieces of it together.

EDWARD.

You promised once, to tell me a story of a poor Indian woman, who suffered a great deal because she did not know this way of making a fire.

MOTHER.

I did so: and as we have finished our thirteenth class, you shall hear it now, though it has no immediate relation to Botany; for it shows the value of knowledge and ingenuity in time of distress. I read the account in Hearne's Journey to the Northern Ocean.

When some of Hearne's companions were hunting, in one of the wildest parts of North America, they observed the track of a strange snow-shoe—

EDWARD.

What sort of a shoe is that?

MOTHER.

It is made of an oblong wooden rim, with cords woven like a net, from side to side, something like the rackets with which you play, but much longer and wider than the foot; it is fastened to the soles of the feet, and is used to prevent the person who wears it from sinking in the soft snow.

The party followed the track, and came at last to a little hut, where they discovered a young woman sitting alone. They soon found that she understood their language, and was one of a western tribe of Indians, who, with some others, had been taken prisoners by another tribe. The savages, according to their custom, surprised her party in the night; and her father, mother, husband, and even her young child, who was only five months old, were put to death. This act of cruelty gave her such an abhorrence of those Indians, although she herself was treated with great kindness, that she resolved to escape from them, and, if possible, to return to her own country, at the hazard of the greatest misery and danger. She succeeded in escaping; but the windings of the rivers and lakes were so numerous, that she lost her way, and was obliged, with her own hands, to build the hut in which she was found, to give her shelter during the winter.

From her account of the number of moons that had pased since her escape, (for that was her way of reckoning time,) it appeared that she had been near seven months without seeing a human face: during all which time she had supported herself very well by snaring partridges, rabbits, and squirrels.

The methods practised by this poor creature to procure a subsistence were truly admirable. When the few deers' sinews that she had taken with her were all used, in making snares for game, and sewing her clothes, she had nothing to supply their place but the sinews of the rabbits' legs and feet; these she twisted together with great dexterity; and the wild animals that she caught not only supplied her with food, but she had made of their skins, a suit of neat and warm clothing for the winter.

Five or six inches of an iron hoop, made into a sort of knife, and the iron head of an arrow, which served her as an awl, were the only tools this poor woman had; but with these she had contrived to make herself complete snow-shoes, and many other useful articles. It would scarcely be imagined, that a person in her forlorn situation could be so composed, as to contrive or execute any thing that was not absolutely necessary to existence; but all her clothing, besides being calculated for real service, showed great taste and even variety of ornament.

Her hours of leisure from hunting had been employed in twisting the inner bark or rind of willows into small lines like twine, of which she had prepared several hundred yards; and of this she intended, as the spring advanced, to have made a fishing net, after the manner of her country.

One of her greatest difficulties was to make a fire, for she had no other materials for that purpose than two hard stones; but by rubbing or striking these together for a long time, she obtained a few sparks, and at last succeeded in kindling some touchwood.

EDWARD.

Is that the wood of the anotta tree, that you told me of?

MOTHER.

No; touchwood is not the produce of any particular tree, but dry decayed wood, of almost any kind, which is used to catch the sparks struck from steel or iron by a flint. I suppose that the poor woman found, by accident, some pieces of this description, and struck out sparks upon them from the two hard stones; but as this method was very laborious and uncertain, she was obliged to keep her fire burning, with great anxiety, through the whole winter.

CONVERSATION THE THIRTEENTH.

CLASS 14. DIDYNAMIA. — NATURAL ORDERS. — GLECHOMA HEDERACEA, GROUND IVY, EXAMINED. — OTHER PLANTS OF THIS CLASS. — FOREIGN TREES. — SITUATION AND DISTRIBUTION OF PLANTS. — EFFECTS OF LIGHT.

MOTHER.

I HAVE already told you, Edward, that the flowers, of the fourteenth class, Didynamia, contain four stamens, two of which are long and two short. But, besides these distinctions, this class is known by some others, which it is important to attend to, that form what is called a natural character.

EDWARD.

What does that mean?

MOTHER.

Some plants, although belonging to different genera, bear so strong a resemblance to each other, in their structure and appearance, that botanists have been enabled to arrange them into sets or groups, which they call Natural Orders: and the circumstances that distinguish these, are called the Natural Character; because they form distinctions which nature itself seems to point out.—Whereas the classes and orders that depend upon the number of the stamens and pistils, though they afford a very convenient method of finding out the names of plants, may be called artificial; for they sometimes separate plants that are in reality very like each other. The umbelliferous plants, for example, have a very obvious natural character. The lilies, too, of which the orange and white lilies in the garden are good examples, form a very distinct natural family; and may easily be known from other tribes, by their bulbous roots, long slender leaves, and handsome flowers, and by having either no calyx, or instead of one a sheath.

EDWARD.

But the hyacinth and tulip are very like what you describe, as well as the lilies.

MOTHER.

So they are; and from this general resemblance, they are placed in the same natural order, and the whole together are called liliaceous plants.

The grasses form another natural tribe, which

includes all plants that have a straight hollow stem, without branches, and commonly jointed: a single undivided leaf, part of which surrounds the stem like a sheath, growing from each joint; and each flower bearing but one seed. Plants that have these characters, whatever be the class in which Linnæus has placed them, belong to the natural order of grasses, called in Latin Gramina. The different species of rush, and the rice plant, though placed in the sixth class of Linnæus because they have six stamens, belong to this natural order, as well as the various kinds of corn and the sugar-cane, which have only three; and this separation of genera that are so much alike, is one of the principal defects of the Linnæan system.

EDWARD.

But is there no arrangement better than Linnæus's?

MOTHER.

Several different systems or arrangements of plants have been invented by other botanists; which are founded, some upon the fruit, some upon the corolla, and others upon the general appearance of the whole plant, without regard to the number of stamens and pistils. There is not any one quite free from objections; but the ingenuity of some of them will interest and delight you very much, when you are sufficiently acquainted with the structure of plants to understand them.

My reasons for having chosen the system of Linnæus, in preference to any other, were, that it is almost universally understood and used in England; and that it will enable you to find out the genera and species of plants, with greater ease and certainty than any other; which is all that I propose to instruct you in at present.

But we must come back to the class Didynamia: and we shall now examine the common ground ivy, which is a good example of it. [See [illegible] There are two orders in this class, the first called Gymnosper'mia, with the seeds naked: the second, Angiosper'mia, having the seeds covered. Pull out one of the blossoms, and tell me to which of these the ground ivy belongs.

EDWARD.

I suppose it is in the first order; for I can see four little seeds in the bottom of the cup, without any covering. But what were the two little white crosses that I saw in the blossom?

MOTHER.

They were the anthers; but you must not be too sure of their number, until you have opened the blossom; you will then find, that what you took for a cross, is in reality composed of

Glechóma hederácea _ *Ground Ivy.*

Class XIV. *DIDYNAMIA* _ Order *GYMNOSPERMIA.*

Hilton

two parts, so shaped, that when they meet in the middle, they look like one little cross. It is this that constitutes the principal distinction of the genus Glecho'ma, to which our plant belongs; and we shall now try, whether the remaining characters correspond with the description.

The cup is small, in proportion to the size of the blossom, and formed of one leaf, with five unequal divisions, each of which ends in a point. The upper lip of the blossom is upright, and slightly notched in the middle; the lower lip is large, turns down, and has three divisions, the middle one the broadest, and notched at the end. The style is thread shaped, and the summit cloven into two pointed divisions. There is no seed-vessel, but the seeds are placed at the bottom of the cup, without any covering, as you have seen. All this agrees so well with our specimen, that there can be no doubt about the genus.

There is but one native species of Glecho'ma, the hedera'cea; and it may be distinguished from the foreign ones by the leaves, which, you perceive, are nearly kidney-shaped, and scolloped at the edges: when rubbed on the under side, they have a pleasant smell, but the upper side has none. It is said that other plants which grow near the ground ivy do not flourish.

You can now probably, understand the natural character of this class; which consists in the calyx being formed of one leaf, like a tube, with five divisions, and being permanent, or remaining upon the stalk until the seeds are ripe. The blossom is of one petal, the lower part like a tube, and the border is divided into two parts like lips; from which last circumstance the flowers belonging to the class are called labiate or lipped, and some of them, from their resemblance to an open mouth, are said to gape or grin. In most instances, the upper lip is like a hood or helmet, and the lower one spreads out, and is divided into three segments.

The plants of the order Gymnospermia are almost universally odoriferous, and none of them are poisonous. Lavender, Laven'dula spi'ca; several species of mint, Men'tha; common marjoram, Orig'anum vulga're; balm, Melis'sa; white horehound, Marru'bium vul'gare; and Vervain, Verbe'na officina'lis; are amongst them; and all are natives of England, except the lavender, which came originally from the south of Europe.

Some of the plants in the second order, Angiospermia, are poisonous; and the common Foxglove, Digita'lis purpu'rea, which grows plentifully in England, though very useful in medicine, is one of these.

There are but few trees in the class Didynamia, and none of them are natives of this country. The calabash-tree, Crescen'tia, of which there are two species, the oval and the round fruited, Crescen'tia Cuje'te, and Crescen'tia cucurbiti'na, is in the order Angiospermia. Both the species are natives of the West-Indies, and are easily propagated by seed. The wood of the tree is hard and smooth, and is used for making different kinds of furniture. The fruit varies in size from two inches to a foot in diameter: The pulp is seldom eaten, except by cattle in time of drought; but the small shells of the long-fruited species, are formed into spoons and ladles; and those of the round fruit into cups. The large shells, which sometimes hold fifteen pints, serve for boiling water in, and will bear the fire as well as earthen pots.

EDWARD.

I think you have told me of very few trees that are natives of England, in comparison with other countries.

MOTHER.

When you consider how very small a part of the world England occupies, you cannot be surprised that the native trees are comparatively few in number: and I ought to have mentioned to you before, that the proportion of trees to herbaceous plants, is much more considerable in the countries near the equator, than towards the poles. But it is singular, that in some parts of North America, though the climate is colder than that of England, the vegetation is richer. In the United States alone, it is supposed that more species are found, of the single genus, Quercus, or oak, than there are of different native trees in the whole of Europe.

Trees grow in such amazing profusion in many parts of North America, that great pains are taken to destroy them. The ground cannot be tilled, nor can the inhabitants support themselves, until they are removed; and the person who can cut down the largest number, and make the fields about his house most free from them, is looked upon as making the greatest improvements in the country. I have heard, that when some Americans landed on a part of the north-west coast of Ireland, which we should consider as very desolate and dreary, they expressed the greatest surprise and pleasure, at the beauty and improved state of a country, "so clear of trees."

EDWARD.

What curious things you tell me. I thought, at first, that botany would teach me only the names and shape of plants.

MOTHER.

You will find, as you advance, that what relates to the particular situations in which vegetables grow, and their distribution in different countries, is very interesting. Some species, for instance, are confined to exceedingly narrow limits, while others are almost universally diffused over the world. A species of marjoram, (Orig'anum Tournefor'tii, a plant in the class Didynamia,) discovered by Tournefort a celebrated French botanist, in the year 1700, upon one rock only in the little island of Amorgos, in the Archipelago, was found, eighty years afterwards, by Sibthorpe another botanist, on the same island, and even upon the very same rock; but no one has ever yet observed it any where else.

Some plants grow wild on mountains only, and are called Alpine, from the word Alps, which signifies high mountainous districts: some grow in vallies only, others upon plains, and some are entirely confined to water, and therefore called aquatic. Some require the hottest climates, some temperate ones, while others thrive no where but in the midst of ice.

Light also, as well as heat, has a great effect upon the colour and growth of plants, so that when they are deprived of it they become white or colourless, and shoot up into pale weak stalks. I have myself seen plants, which had grown in dark rooms or cellars, and were perfectly white, gradually become green on being exposed to the light.

EDWARD.

Then does the gardener cover up endive and celery with earth, to make them grow white?

MOTHER.

He does, my dear; and earthing them up in this manner, is called blanching.

Trees show how beneficial the influence of light is to them, by their branches being generally thicker and more full of leaves on the side exposed to the sun, than on the opposite one. The knowledge of this circumstance is very useful to the Laplanders; who being unacquainted with the compass, would lose their way in their long journies, through wild districts without roads or paths, if they were not guided by various natural appearances, that enable them to distinguish the points of north and south.

CONVERSATION THE FOURTEENTH.

CLASS 15. — TETRADYNAMIA. — ORDERS. — CHEIRANTHUS CHEIRI, COMMON WALL-FLOWER, EXAMINED. — CLASS 16. MONADELPHIA. — ORDERS. — MALVA SYLVESTRIS, COMMON MALLOW, EXAMINED. — YEW TREE. — PINES; THEIR VARIOUS USES. — COTTON PLANT.

MOTHER.

I HOPE, Edward, that we can examine two plants to-day, which I know will give you pleasure; for I have not much to tell you about the fifteenth class, Tetradynamia. Do you recollect how it is distinguished?

EDWARD.

The flowers contain six stamens, four of them long, and two short.

MOTHER.

You are quite right; but as the difference of their length is not always very striking, and the plants of the sixth class contain the same number of stamens, it will save you trouble to remember, that the flowers of the class Hexandria never have four petals, while those of the fifteenth class always have that number. The last are generaly called cruciform or cross-shaped, from the four petals being so placed as to form a kind of cross; and this circumstance forms the natural character of the class Tetradynamia.

In moist situations, and during wet seasons, the cruciform plants become acrid, (which signifies having a hot and biting taste, like mustard,) but none of them are poisonous. Even the common turnip, Bras'sica Ra'pa, whose root in a dry sandy soil is so sweet and juicy, becomes, in wet land, hard, and disagreeable to the taste; and the common horse-radish, Cochlea'ria Armora'cia, when growing near water, is so extremely acrid that it can hardly be used.

The orders of this class, you may remember, are two; distinguished from each other by the shape of the seed-vessel, which in both is a pod. In the first order, Siliculosa, the pod is broad and short; and in the second, Siliquosa, long and narrow.

The first order contains about twelve native genera; among which are the sea-kale, Cram'be marit'ima; shepherd's purse, Thlaspi Bursa-pasto'ris; candy-tuft, I'beris ama'ra, (which is very often cultivated in flower-gardens;) and common Whitlow-grass, Dra'ba verna; a pretty little plant, which shows very well the effect of climates upon vegetables; for in Sweden it flowers in the month of April; in Germany, in March; in England, Holland, and France, in February; and in Sicily it is in flower all through the winter.

The second order, Siliquosa, contains about eleven native genera, some of which we use as food. For instance, the common water-cress, Sisym'brium Nastur'tium; the turnip, Bras'sica Ra'pa; cabbage, Bras'sica olera'cea; rape, Bras'sica Na'pus, which is chiefly cultivated for the sake of the oil that is procured from its seeds; mustard, Sina'pis ni'gra; and the radish, Raph'anus Raphanis'trum.

The wall-flower, too, that you may recollect having brought in from the garden, to learn from it the different parts of a flower, is in this second order. It is a good example of the class, and we will now examine its character. [See PLATES 15, and 1.]—

The pods that contain the seeds, you perceive, are long ones; the order therefore is Siliquosa, in which there are two divisions of the genera, one having the calyx open, with the leafits spreading; the other, to which this plant belongs, having a close cup, and the leafits approaching each other at the top. This genus is named Cheiran'thus, and is distinguished from the others, of the same division, principally by two little roundish bodies, called glands, which surround the bottom of the two shorter stamens; but they are not very distinct without the assistance of a magnifying glass. [See Plate 1.] These glands form the nectaries of the wall-flower, as I have already mentioned to you. The cup consists of four upright spear-shaped leafits, of which the two outermost bulge, or swell a little, at the bottom. There are four petals, forming a cross, the claws of which are as long as the cup. The four long stamens are of the same length as the calyx; and the two shorter ones are curved outwards at the lower part, being pushed out, as it were, by the glands that surround them at the bottom. The anthers are long, upright, pointed at top, and cloven at the bottom. The germen is as long as the filaments, and supports a very short style, with a divided summit. The seed-vessel is a long pod, containing several flat egg-shaped seeds.

The specific name of our plant is Chei'ri. It is supposed by several botanists to be a variety of the native species, Fruticulo'sus, and is so common in all our gardens, that I wished to examine it with you. It differs from the plant that grows wild on old walls, and roofs of houses, in having somewhat larger flowers, with petals not of an uniform yellow, but stained with brown or rust colour: the two plants, however, are very nearly alike.

Cheiranthus Cheiri _ *Common Wall Flower.*

Class XV. *TETRADYNAMIA* _ Order *SILIQUOSA.*

Milton sc.

Published April 1.1817. by Longman & Co.

The leaves are spear-shaped, and the stem somewhat shrubby.

There are two other native species of Chei-ran'thus; one of which, the inca'nus, or stock-gilly-flower, is very much cultivated in gardens, but has been found wild only in one place in England. The sinua'tus, or sea-stock, grows upon the sea-shore: and in both these species, the flowers are purplish, and the whole plant is covered with a short whitish down.

EDWARD.

The stem of the wall-flower is so woody, that it is very like a shrub. Is it one?

MOTHER.

No, my dear; but from its having a woody stem, it is called shrub-like. It is a perennial plant, and in old gardens I have seen the stem so thick, and so like wood, that I could almost have mistaken it myself.

We have now done with the class Tetradynamia; and as I am afraid that the character of the sixteenth class, Monadelphia, is not easily remembered, we shall look at your drawing, and go over the description again.

EDWARD.

Here it is, [see PLATE 2]: the filaments are all joined at the bottom, but separate at the top.

MOTHER.

Yes; and the class is called Monadelphia, from two Greek words, which signify one brotherhood. In most of the classes that we have already examined, the orders are determined by the number of pistils; but in this one the number of the stamens determines the order. All the genera hitherto discovered come under eight orders, but only three of them contain plants native in England; Triandria with three stamens, Decandria with ten, and Polyandria with more than twenty.

In this class, the calyx is of the utmost importance, and is the part by which the different genera are principally distinguished.

The order Triandria contains, according to Withering, one native genus; and there is only one native species of it, the Juniper-tree, Junip'erus commu'nis.* The berries of this plant are two years in ripening, and afford an oil, which gives the flavour to gin or juniper-water. The bark is sometimes made into ropes, and the wood is hard and durable. Frankincense, which is the produce of another species, Junip'erus Ly'cia, is brought to this country from Turkey and the East Indies, but principally from Arabia.

The Tamarind-tree, Tamarin'dus In'dica, whose

* Class Dioecia, order Monadelphia, of Linnæus.

fruit is so delightfully acid, is a native of the East and West Indies, and belongs also to this order.

The Gera'nium, of which there are several native species, and a great number of foreign ones, is the only genus in the order Decandria. The species that are found in Africa are much larger, and have far more beautiful flowers, than those which grow in Europe.

There are, according to Withering, five native genera in the order Polyandria; the marsh-mallow, Althæ'a; common mallow, Malva; tree mallow, Lavate'ra; the yew-tree, Tax'us; and the fir or pine tree, Pinus; but the last two genera are in the classes Dioecia and Monoecia of Linnæus.

EDWARD.

I have seen the common mallow so often, that I should like to examine it.

MOTHER.

Well then, bring in some of it, and we will go through the description. You cannot fail to meet with it in the next hedge.

EDWARD.

It appears as if there were two calyxes. [See Plate 16.]

MOTHER.

It has what is called a double calyx, or one

within another; and it is the circumstance of the outer one being composed of three leaves, that constitutes the principal character of the genus Mal'va; Lavăte'ra has an outer cup of one leaf, with three divisions only; and in Althæ'a, (of which the holly-hock in our garden is a Chinese species,) the divisions are nine. The inner cup of the Mal'va is of one leaf, with five shallow divisions. The blossom is composed of five heart-shaped flat petals, united at the bottom to the tube formed by the filaments. The middle of the receptacle rises like a little pillar; and the seed-vessels (which are generally eight in number,) with one seed in each, stand round it in a circle.

There are three or four native species of Mal'va: Ours, which is the sylves'tris, or common mallow, is distinguished from the others, by having a rough, upright, and somewhat woody stem; and hairy leaves, with five or seven divisions, the edges unequally notched, and a dark purplish stain on the lower part of each, near the stalk: the leaf-stalks and fruit-stalks are hairy.

Of the Yew-tree, Tax'us, there is but one species, bacca'ta, native in England, the wood of which is uncommonly hard, tough, smooth when cut, and beautifully veined with red. It is so durable, that it is a common saying, amongst the inhabitants of New-Forest in Hampshire, that a post of yew will outlive a post of iron.

Malva sylvestris _ *Common Mallow.*

Class XVI. *MONADELPHIA* _ Order *POLYANDRIA*.

Milton sc.

Published April 2. 1817 by Longman & Co.

The Pine genus, Pinus *, includes several species; but the only native one is the Scotch Fir, Pinus sylves'tris, which grows plentifully throughout the Highlands of Scotland. When this tree is planted in a grove, the trunk becomes tall and naked, but in open sunny places it sends off many branches. It is said to live sometimes to the age of four hundred years. The wood, which is called red deal, is very smooth and light. The bark will tan leather, and in years of scarcity it is dried, ground to powder, and made into bread, by the people of the north of Europe. The inhabitants of the Scottish Highlands dig up the roots, and divide them into small splinters, to burn instead of candles; for they contain a great quantity of resin, and easily take fire.

The Black Spruce, Pinus ni'gra, is a native of North America. The young shoots of this species are used for making spruce beer.

The Cedar of Lebanon, Pinus Ce'drus, grows on mountains in the Levant, especially on the celebrated Mount Lebanon, from which it takes its name. The wood is not destroyed by insects, in consequence of its bitter taste, which they cannot endure; and for this reason the ancients used tablets of cedar, to write upon, and smeared their books and writings with a juice drawn from the wood, to pre-

* Class Monoecia, order Monadelphia, of Linnæus.

serve them. Solomon's temple and palace, it is supposed, were built of this wood.

The Larch-tree, Pinus la'rix, is a native of the Alps and Appenines, where it sometimes grows to the height of nearly two hundred feet. The wood is said to be more durable even than oak, and has the valuable property of not warping or shrinking; it was used by painters more than any other, before the use of canvas became general. Several of Raphael's pictures are painted on boards of larch.

The Norway Pine, Pinus a'bies, affords the wood called white deal, that is employed for so many useful purposes in England. It is from the sap of this species that pitch, tar, common resin, and turpentine are obtained. You will find an account of the method of preparing these different substances very curious.

EDWARD.

Are there are any other useful plants in this class, besides the pines?

MOTHER.

That which produces cotton is the principal one that I recollect: the botanical name of the genus is Gossyp'ium, and all the species at present known are natives of the East and West Indies. What we call cotton, is a soft downy substance that surrounds the seeds; which, in one species, Gossy'pium herba'ceum, the common cotton, is of a snowy white: but in the species Barbaden'se, which grows in great perfection in the Chinese province of Kiang-nan, (of which Nankin is the capital city,) it is, in its natural state, of a yellow colour inclining to red; and the kind of cloth called Nankin, which is made of it in that country, is of great value, because it is very strong, and fades very little, even after long use and frequent washing.

CONVERSATION THE FIFTEENTH.

CLASS 17. DIADELPHIA. — PAPILIONACEOUS FLOWERS. — POD AND LEGUMEN. — LOTUS CORNICULATUS, BIRD'S-FOOT CLOVER, EXAMINED. — TREFOILS. — FURZE. — INDIGO. — MOVING PLANT. — ACACIA TREE. — CLASS 18. POLYADELPHIA. — HYPERICUM ANDROSÆMUM, COMMON TUTSAN, EXAMINED. — ORANGE AND LEMON TREES.

EDWARD.

I THINK I can tell you the character of the seventeenth class, Diadelphia: the filaments are all united in two sets.

MOTHER.

That is certainly the character given by Linnæus: but some other circumstances must be attended to, besides the connection of the stamens and number of the sets; for the flowers of different genera in this class differ from each other in these respects; some having the filaments united in one set only. The shape of the blossom will enable you to decide in doubtful cases; for it is always irregular, that is, the petals are unequal and of different figures; and in general it has some resemblance to a butterfly, like the sweet-pea blossom that you see in the garden; for which reason the flowers of this class are called Papilionaceous, from the word Papilio, the Latin for a butterfly. In flowers of this shape, the number of stamens is most commonly ten; which in some instances are all quite distinct, and then, of course, the plant belongs to the class Decandria: but whenever you meet with a flower shaped like a butterfly, if any of the filaments are joined together, you may be sure that it belongs to Diadelphia.

The Orders of this class depend upon the number of the stamens; which are either five, six, eight, or ten. The last number is by far the most common; nine of the stamens being generally united, and the tenth standing by itself.

You will understand better what I have said about the shape of the flowers, when we have examined a plant of this class; and I think I have seen one in the meadow near the gardener's house. Let us go out and look for it.

EDWARD.

Here is a very pretty plant, that has a blossom something like what you have just told me of; but the flower is so different from those we have already examined, that I don't think I can understand the parts, by myself.

MOTHER.

The shape of the blossom in this class is so peculiar, that its petals, which are five, are called by different names. Take off one of the flowers, and I will show them to you. [See PLATE 17.] This large uppermost one, that turns backwards, is called the Standard; the two next, which are both alike, and placed one on each side, are the Wings; the lowermost, between the wings, is called the boat or Keel, and is generally composed of one hollow petal, but sometimes of two: this contains within it the stamens and pistil, which it defends from rain. Do you think you can find the germen or seed-vessel?

EDWARD.

I believe I can; but it is not very distinct.

MOTHER.

You will find it more so in the plants that have shed their petals; but for the unripe ones, you must use your magnifying-glass.

EDWARD.

Is it not a pod? It is something like the seed-vessel of the wall-flower, and is full of little seeds.

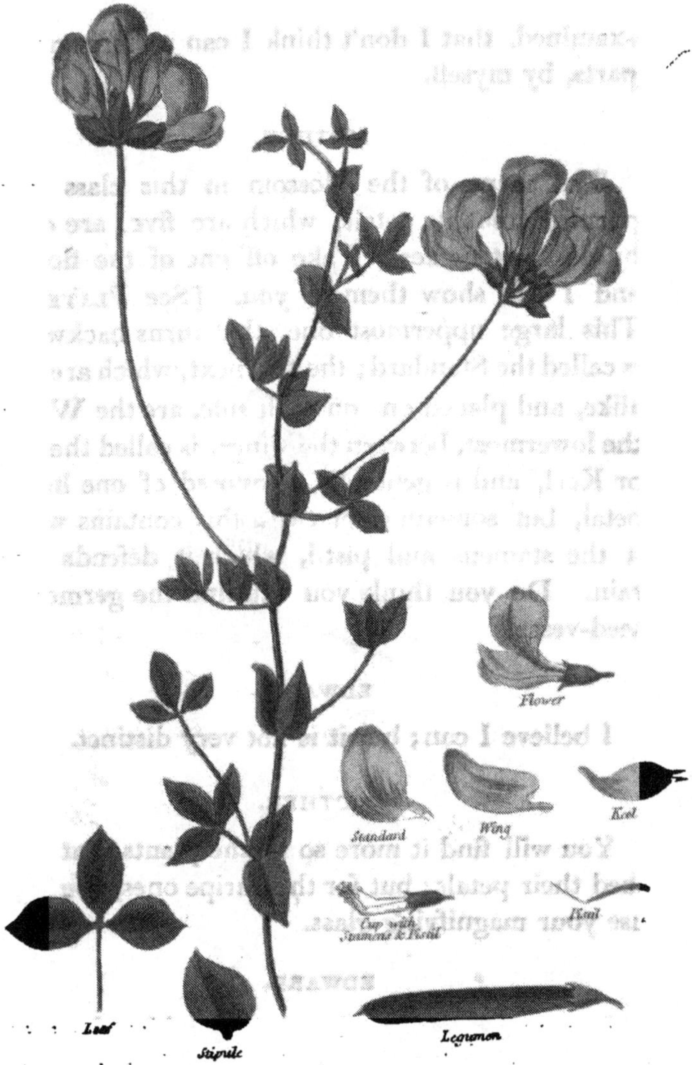

Lótus corniculátus _ *Birds foot Trefoil*.

Class XVII *DIADELPHIA* ___ Order *DECANDRIA*.

Milton sc.

Published April 2 1817. by Longman & Co.

MOTHER.

It is something like a pod; but there is a remarkable difference, which you must remember. In the seed-vessel of the wall-flower, you recollect, there was a partition between the two outer shells; upon both sides of which the seeds were arranged, being fixed alternately to different edges: but in this seed-vessel, (and you will see the same thing more plainly in the common pea,) there is no partition; and all the seeds are fastened to one of the seams, in such a manner, that when the seed-vessel is opened, they lie alternately in the two shells. I have made a drawing to explain this to you more distinctly.

Pod, with one side opened.

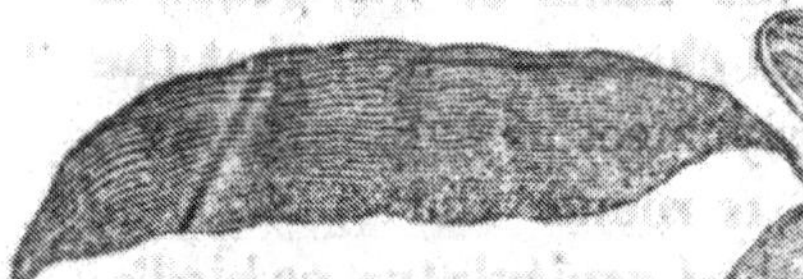

Legumen.

Legumen opened.

This last kind of seed-vessel is called a Legumen; and the plants that bear it, are said to be

Leguminous. Very few of them are poisonous; indeed most of them produce very wholesome food for man and the larger animals; but there is one found in the West Indies, called Jamaica Dog-wood, or Fish-bean, Piscid'ia erythri'na, the leaves and branches of which, when thrown into water where there are fish, have such an effect upon them, that they come up and float upon the surface, and may be easily taken with the hand.

But let us examine our plant.—If you reckon the stamens (which are of different lengths), you will find that there are ten; nine of them united together at the lower part, into a sort of membrane, which covers the germen. The order, then, is Decandria; and this contains so many genera, that, for convenience, it is subdivided into six sets, four of which depend, chiefly, upon the shape and structure of the legumen. This plant belongs to the division, that has a legumen of one cell containing several seeds: the name of the genus is Lo'tus; and the principal characters are, that the wings of the flower nearly meet at the upper part, and that the legumen is round and full. The species that we have, is the Cornícula'tus, or bird's-foot clover; which is distinguished, by the heads of flowers being flat at the top, and consisting of a small number only; the legumens spreading out like the spokes of a wheel; and the stems generally trailing on the ground. The leaves have three divisions, of an oblong shape: and where they spring from the stalks, there are two little leaves, called stipules, that are of a different figure from the divisions of the leaf itself. The flowers, before they open, are of a red colour; but when expanded, of a rich yellow. The plant varies very much in different situations: it is commonly decumbent, or grows near the ground; but in meadows it is often upright, like this specimen.

The Lo'tus is one genus of a very numerous tribe of plants, that are in general called trefoils, from the genus Trifo'lium, (which signifies three-leaved), because each leaf looks like three. The common English name is Clover, and almost all the kinds are of great value to farmers, for they afford good pasture for cattle, and make excellent hay.

EDWARD.

I think I have often seen both purple and white clover; but I did not think the flowers looked as if they were butterfly-shaped.

MOTHER.

I dare say, that you supposed each Head of clover to be a single flower; but if you examine one, you will soon find that it consists of a great number of small flowers; each of which has its own little calyx, and as perfect a blossom as that of the lotus, composed of a standard, two wings, and a keel. But you must look at them through your magnifying-glass, if you wish to see the stamens and pistils distinctly.

EDWARD.

How pretty the little flowers must be! When I go out to day I will gather some clover, and examine it. — Are the pease and beans, that we eat, in this class, as well as the sweet-pea in the garden?

MOTHER.

They are, my dear; and in the order Decandria also; as are likewise the kidney-bean, Phase'olus vulga'ris; the vetch, Vicia; wild liquorice, Astrag'alus; and saintfoin, Hedys'arum. The botanical name of the pea is Pi'sum, and the species that we eat is the sati'vum, of which there are several varieties; the bean is a species of vetch, Vicia faba: but neither of the last-mentioned species are natives of England. The pea came originally from the south of Europe; and a great many varieties of the seed have been produced by cultivation, which differ very much from each other in size and flavour. The bean is a native of Egypt.

The common broom, Spar'tium scopa'rium, belongs to this class, and grows wild in England, as well as the furze, Ulex Europæ'us, that you see in such large bushes on the heath. This last shrub, though it is so abundant in England, is by no means common in other parts of Europe:

Portugal and France produce it more plentifully, perhaps, than any other country except our own. When Linnæus came to England, in the year 1736, he was so much delighted with the golden bloom of the furze, which he saw for the first time on the commons near London, that it is said, he fell on his knees in raptures at the sight.

In Cornwall this plant grows, with great luxuriance, to the height of six or eight feet; but it will not bear severe cold. Linnæus tried to preserve some plants of it through the winter in Sweden, under cover, with as much care as we bestow on hot-house plants, but without success.

The remaining plants of the class Diadelphia, that I shall mention to you, are not natives of England.

That which affords the indigo, with which blue cloth is dyed, Indigo'fera tincto'ria (Diadelphia Decandria), is a native of the East-Indies. The dye is a light solid substance, somewhat like starch, but of a deep blue colour; and is obtained, by steeping the leaves and small branches of the plant in water, and drying the sediment which they deposit. All the species of Indigo'fera afford it, which is the case also with several other leguminous plants. The leaves of the Lo'tus cornicula'tus, as they dry, become blue.

There is a foreign species of saintfoin, called the Moving-plant, Hedydys'arum gy'rans (of a genus belonging to this class), which is a very extraordinary production. It grows on the banks of the river Ganges, near Bengal, in the East-Indies. Its leaves possess the property of moving spontaneously, or without being touched; sometimes one of them will move suddenly, while the rest remain still; and at other times they all move together, or separately, without any regularity. You will find hereafter, that there are several other marks of a sort of feeling, among plants of different tribes. The leaves of the trefoils always fold up when rain approaches.

The acacia-tree, Robin'ia pseudoaca'cia, which is so much admired in our shrubberies, has such very brittle wood, that a slight blast of wind is sufficient to break off its branches, and it is consequently not fit for exposed situations; but it makes amends for this defect, by sending up from its roots innumerable suckers, which grow very rapidly. I have read of a farmer, at Long Island in North America, who planted a field of fourteen acres with suckers of this tree, during the year of his marriage, as a provision for his children: his eldest son married at twenty-two years of age; and on that occasion the farmer cut down about three hundred pounds worth of timber, out of his acacia-wood; which he gave his son to buy a farm with. Three years after, he did the same for one of his daughters; and in this way he provided for his whole family. The wood, in the mean time, repairing by its suckers all the losses that it sustained.

We are now, Edward, to begin the eighteenth class, POLYADELPHIA.—

EDWARD.

Is it not in the flowers of this class, that the stamens are united into more than two sets?

MOTHER.

Yes; but in some species, the filaments are so much separated, that unless you examine them quite down to the bottom, you might suppose that they were all distinct, and of course consider the plant as belonging to the class Icosandria, or Polyandria.

The Orders, according to Linnæus, depend upon the number of the *Stamens*, and the plant that I have chosen for you to examine [See PLATE 18.] belongs to the third order, Polyandria; which contains plants with very numerous stamens, not connected with the calyx.

In the genus Hyper'icum (the only genus of native plants in this class), the calyx is placed below the germen, and has five divisions; the petals are five in number, and blunt at the ends; the stamens are very numerous, like hairs, and united at the base into three or five sets, corresponding with the number of the styles; the capsule contains several seeds, and is round, and divided also into as many cells as there are styles.

This species of Hyper'icum, the Androsæ'mum, though not common in England, happens to grow in our neighbourhood, and shows the character of the class very distinctly. It may be known from the others, by having three pistils, a shrub-like stem with two edges, and fruit consisting of a pulpy berry, which is black when ripe. The flower is large, and of a rich yellow colour; and the plant grows naturally in woods, and in damp ground under hedges.

One of the most remarkable foreign genera of this class, and of this order also, is the Ci'trus; of which the orange and lemon trees, Ci'trus auran-tium and Ci'trus med'ica, are species. These trees are very handsome evergreens, and are frequently cultivated in green-houses, in England; but they are generally much smaller with us than in their native country, the warmer parts of Asia, where they grow to the height of twelve or fifteen feet.

Berry

Hypericum Androsæmum _ *Tutsan*.

Class XVIII. *POLYADELPHIA* Order *POLYANDRIA*.

Milton sc

Published April 1 1817, by Longman & Co.

CONVERSATION THE SIXTEENTH.

CLASS 19. SYNGENESIA. — STRUCTURE OF A COMPOUND FLOWER. — NATURAL CHARACTER OF THIS CLASS. — CALYX, SEEDS, AND DOWN. — ORDERS. — BELLIS PERENNIS, COMMON DAISY, EXAMINED. — OTHER PLANTS OF THIS CLASS.

MOTHER.

I HAVE brought in a daisy, Edward, for you to examine this morning; and before I tell you any thing of the nineteenth class, Syngenesia, to which it belongs, we will try to find out how the flowers are constructed. [See PLATE 19.] At first, you perceive, they do not look like any of those that you have already examined.

EDWARD.

No, indeed. There is a sort of cup, and a great many white and pink petals; but instead of stamens and pistils in the middle, I see only a great number of yellow dots. What are they?

MOTHER.

Pull off all the parts that are within the cup, and look at them again, with your magnifying glass.

EDWARD.

Oh! now I see that the yellow spots were the tops of beautiful little things like flowers; and these, I suppose, are seeds, below them.

MOTHER.

Well; now I shall open one of these little flowers with my needle; (for it requires some practice, and you cannot do it so readily yourself.) Can you perceive with your glass, that each little blossom is shaped like a funnel, with five divisions in its border? The stamens are so small, in the daisy, that you can hardly see them; but in larger flowers of this class, you will find that they are five in number, with the filaments distinct, but the anthers joined together, side by side, like a tube; a single pistil, with a notched summit passing up through them, and an egg-shaped seed below.

EDWARD.

How very beautiful it is!

MOTHER.

Now look at what you called the white and pink

petals, and try if you can describe one of them as they appear to you.

EDWARD.

They look like little blossoms too, but they are very different from the yellow ones. There is a long white part, tipped with red, coming out from one side; and the blossom looks as if the other petals had been torn off.

MOTHER.

The white part is one of the divisions in the border of the little blossom, but much longer than the rest; you see it is shaped something like the head of a spear, blunted, with a very slight notch at the end: and you will find, with your glass, that the other part of the border, which you thought was torn, has three very small teeth. Upon opening the blossom, you perceive that there are no stamens, but the style comes up from the seed through the tube of the blossom itself, and has two summits curled a little backwards. There is no seed-vessel; but the seeds, as in the little yellow flower that we have just examined, are single, naked, shaped somewhat like an egg a little flattened, and placed immediately below the blossom. Now, if you look at the receptacle, from which we pulled off all these little flowers, you will find that it stands up like a sugar-loaf in the middle of the cup, and is dotted all over with little holes; these are the places in which the seeds were fixed: and when I cut down through the sugar-loaf, you see that it has a soft pith within. [See Plate 19.]

EDWARD.

And is every daisy that we see in the fields, made like this, of so many beautiful little flowers?

MOTHER.

All the flowers of this class, not only the daisy, but the dandelion, the thistle, and a great number of the most common wild flowers, are formed nearly in the same way; and their separate parts, when highly magnified, are equally beautiful and curious. But there are differences in their shape and arrangement, that enable botanists to divide the class into orders and genera, which you will now be able to understand. I shall, however, give you only a general explanation of them; for I do not advise you to examine many plants of this class, until you are better acquainted with those that have larger and more simple flowers.

The class Syngenesia, comprehends the flowers which botanists call compound,—that is, which are composed, like the daisy, of a number of small flowers or florets, all placed upon the same receptacle, and within one common calyx: the stamens

PLATE 19

Flower cut down to show the Receptacle

Floret of Center

Floret of Circumference

Magnified

being five in number, with distinct filaments; but the anthers united side by side, so as to form a little tube.

The compound flowers are all so far alike, that this class has a very perfect natural character, which their general resemblance to the daisy will sufficiently point out to you, when you meet any of them: but the calyx and seeds, in particular, are worth your attending to.

The calyx consists, sometimes of a single row of leaves or scales; sometimes of two rows, as in the daisy; and in some flowers, as in the common artichoke, the scales are placed over each other, alternately, like tiles upon the roof of a house. The calyx, in many instances, opens as the florets expand, and closes when they fall off, as if to confine the young seeds; but it opens again to make room for the seeds, as they ripen and increase in size; and in some plants turns quite back, to let them escape. The dandelion and coltsfoot are in this last state, when you see their heads covered with down.

The seeds are, in several species, very remarkable; they are placed below the corolla, and there is never more than one to each floret. In many instances, they are tipped with a beautiful sort of down, consisting of a great number of spokes placed in a circle; these spokes are sometimes branched or feathered; and in some cases, as in the common dandelion, the entire wheel is fixed upon a sort of stem or pillar, which is itself fastened to the seed.

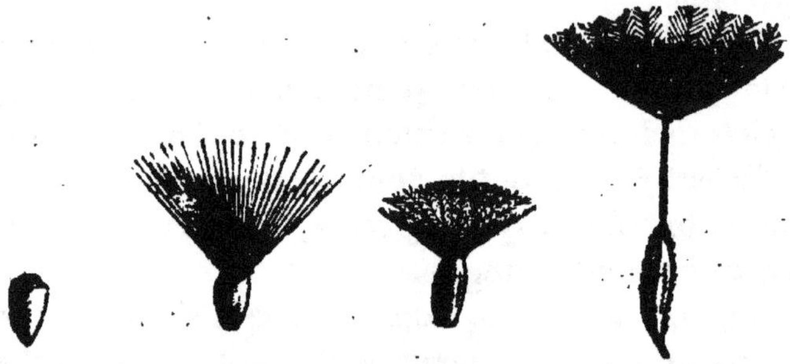

Seed. Simple Down. Feathered Down. Feathered Down on a pillar.

The down is a beautiful object for the microscope, and its use is very important; for it enables the wind to carry the seeds to considerable distances from the plant, and as it were to sow them, in situations which otherwise they might never have reached.

EDWARD.

The down of the coltsfoot is very soft like cotton. Is it ever made any use of?

MOTHER.

I have heard of its being used for making tinder. The poor people in the highlands of Scotland stuff pillows with the down of several different plants.

The Orders in this class, are founded upon the

manner in which the florets of different kinds are disposed in the compound flowers: for they may be all of one kind; or there may be some of one sort in the centre, and others of different structure in the circumference, or border, of the flower.

In the first order, called Polygamia equalis, all the florets have both stamens and pistils; and each floret has one seed.

In the second order, Polygamia superflua, the florets of the centre have both stamens and pistils; but those of the border, pistils only: and all have seeds.

In the third order, Polygamia frustranea, the florets of the centre have both stamens and pistils; but those of the circumference have neither.

In the fourth order, Polygamia necessaria, the florets of the centre have stamens only, without seeds; and those of the border have pistils only, with seeds.

In the fifth order, Polygamia segregata, the flowers are not constructed quite as in the rest. The florets have all five stamens, with united anthers, and are all included in one general calyx; but each floret has, besides, a little calyx of its own. Of this order there is no native genus.

EDWARD.

am afraid it will be a long time before

I know this class well; for the orders appear more difficult to understand, than those of the other classes.

MOTHER.

You will soon find, that the experience you gain, by examining a few plants yourself, will remove whatever you now suppose to be a difficulty, and give you more instruction than any thing that I can tell you.

The chief thing to be attended to, in the class Syngenesia, is the union of the anthers; for there are some flowers in the other classes, which at first you might suppose to belong to it, but whose stamens are not united: and with regard to the orders, it is only necessary to observe how the florets containing the stamens and pistils are disposed in the compound flower.

Now let us go on to the generic and specific characters of our daisy. — The florets in the centre of the flower have both stamens and pistils; but those in the circumference pistils only; it is then in the second order, Polygamia superflua. The name of the genus is Bel'lis; which is distinguished from the other genera, of the same order, by the receptacle being conical, without hair or bristles; the calyx roundish; and the seeds egg-shaped, and without down. There is only one native species, the Peren'nis, or common daisy: and its distinctions from the foreign species are, that the flower-stalks have no leaves, each supporting a single flower; and that the root is creeping, or spreading to some distance, and putting forth fibres. The daisy is in blow almost all the year round, but shuts up its flowers every night, and on the approach of rainy weather.

You can never fail to procure plants in this class, for it is a very numerous one, and contains several that grow wild in England. Among others the dandelion, Leon'todon tarax'acum; burdock, Arc'tium lap'pa; thistle, Car'duus; tansey, Tanace'tum vulga're; coltsfoot, Tussila'go far'fara; groundsel, Sene'cio vulga'ris; and chamomile, An'themis nob'ilis. Of these, the dandelion is perhaps the most common, growing on rubbish and all uncultivated land, as well as in meadows, where you have seen it, and bearing flowers the greater part of the year. In France, this plant is very much used in sallad; and at Gottingen, the roots are roasted and used like coffee by the poorer inhabitants. The juice of the roots and leaves is employed as a medicine in this country.

The artichoke, Cyn'ara scol'ymus, and sun-flower, Helian'thus, of which there are several species, belong also to the class Syngenesia. The artichoke is a native of the south of Europe, where it is much more generally used than with us, and is even eaten raw with salt and pepper. The common sun-flower, Helian'thus annuus, grows wild in Mexico and Peru; and the Jerusalem artichoke, another species, Helian'thus tubero'sus, is a native of Brazil.

It is remarkable, that yellow is the prevailing colour in the flowers of this class; and that, although most of the plants are bitter, none of them are poisonous, except, perhaps, the wild lettuce, Lactu'ca viro'sa, when it grows in shady situations.

CONVERSATION THE SEVENTEENTH.

THE FOUR CLASSES OMITTED BY WITHERING. — CLASS 20. GYNANDRIA. — NATURAL ORDER, ORCHIDEÆ. — CLASS 21, MONOECIA. — BREAD FRUIT TREE. — MAIZE. — COCOA-NUT. — INDIAN RUBBER. — TALLOW-TREE. — OTHER VALUABLE TREES. — CLASS 22. DIOECIA. — WILLOWS. — DATE-PALM. — PISTACHIA-TREE. — HEMP. — NUTMEG. — CLASS 23. POLYGAMIA. — PLANTAIN-TREE. — SENSITIVE-PLANT. — FIG.

MOTHER.

You will be sorry to hear, Edward, that we have no plant to examine to-day.

EDWARD.

But there are twenty-four classes; and we have gone through only nineteen?

MOTHER.

Very true; but you may remember my having told you, that Dr. Withering, in his arrangement of British plants, has distributed those of the twentieth, twenty-first, twenty-second, and twenty-third classes, among the first nineteen; according to the number of their stamens. And although this disposition of them has not been approved of by some very good botanists, I have thought it better, for the reason I have mentioned, to follow it, in speaking of the native plants of England.

The plants of foreign countries, however, are universally arranged according to the original method of Linnæus; and some of these are so curious and useful, that I wish to mention a few of them to you. Look at your drawing of the classes, [See PLATE 2.], and you will find a short character of the four omitted by Dr. Withering: their names are Gynandria, Monoecia, Dioecia, and Polygamia.

In the twentieth class, GYNANDRIA, the stamens grow upon the pistil itself, either on the style or germen; and the orders depend upon their number. The plants which have this character the most distinctly, belong to a natural tribe called Orchid'eæ, which includes, besides other genera, the Or'chises, of which there are a good many native species. I have drawn the flower of one of these, in the table of the classes, that will give you an idea of the general appearance of the tribe; but as their structure is not easily understood, I shall not at present say any thing more about them.

All the flowers of the classes Monoecia and

Dioecia, and some of those in Polygamia, are imperfect; that is, they want either stamens or pistils.

In the twenty-first, MONOECIA, some of the flowers have stamens only, and others, on the same plant, only pistils; but none of them have both. The class contains a number of curious and important genera.

The Bread-fruit-tree, Artocar'pus inci'sa, which is very valuable to the inhabitants of the South-Sea Islands, belongs to one of these genera. It grows to the height of about forty feet, and the fruit, which is as large as a child's head, hangs upon the boughs like apples. The eatable part lies between the skin and the core, and is very white, soft, and of the consistence of new bread, with a sweetish taste, like that of the Jerusalem artichoke; but it must be roasted before it is eaten. It is in season for about seven months of the year, and during the whole of that time supplies very wholesome and agreeable food to the inhabitants of the islands; who also make cloth of the bark of the tree, and use the wood in building their huts and canoes. There is another species of this plant, the Artocar'pus integrifo'lia, or Indian Jaca-tree, which is a native of the East-Indies: the fruit is said to weigh about thirty pounds, and is used as food, but not so generally as the bread-fruit.

The Maize or Indian corn, Ze'a Mä'ys, (Monoecia Triandria,) is a very useful plant. It is a native of America, and is cultivated in several other countries. The seeds grow in ears, which are very large, each of them bearing about eight rows of grain; and every row contains at least thirty grains, which give much more flour than those of wheat, or any of our kinds of corn. The stalk of the maize is jointed, like the sugar cane or bamboo, and it contains a juice from which a syrup like that of sugar is often made.

The Cocoa-nut-tree, Co'cos nucif'era, was originally a native of the East-Indies, but has been introduced in several other warm countries. It thrives remarkably well on the sea-shore; indeed the neighbourhood of the sea appears to be necessary to its growth: and M. de Humboldt, a celebrated traveller, mentions, that on the banks of the river Oronoco, when the cocoa nut is planted, a quantity of salt is thrown into the hole along with it. The tree grows to the height of sixty feet, and has a fine appearance, the top of the stem being crowned with about fifty leaves, which are from ten to fifteen feet long; with nuts nearly as large as a man's head hanging from it, in clusters of about a dozen each. You have often seen the inner shells of these nuts; which consist of a very hard case, and contain a thick coat of kernel of an agreeable flavour, and a sweet milky liquor. These hard cases are employed with us for making sugar-bowls, and various toys, and are very useful to the natives of the countries where the tree grows.

EDWARD.

You told me yesterday, that the mat at the green-house-door, was made of part of the cocoa-nut. How can that be?

MOTHER.

In their natural state, the inner shells are surrounded with a thick crust of coarse fibres, which are employed for making mats, a purpose that they answer very well; and the nuts have besides a smooth outer rind. The Indians make ropes of the bark of the tree, and use the leaves for making mats, baskets, and brooms.

The wood of the Cypress-tree, Cupres'sus sempervi'rens, (Monoecia Monadelphia,) is said to resist worms and moths remarkably, and to last for many centuries. The chests that contain the Egyptian mummies, are found to be made of it, and the coffins in which the Athenians buried their heroes, were of cypress wood. The doors of Saint Peter's church at Rome were originally made of this timber, and when they were removed, at the end of six hundred years, in order to put gates of brass in their place, they did not show the slightest appearance of decay. In the island of Candia, where these trees grow in abundance, they are so valuable, that one of them is reckoned a daughter's portion.

The tree which produces the Indian rubber or Caoutchouc, is a native of the West-Indies: This substance is an elastic resin of very singular properties; which is deposited by a liquor that oozes out from incisions made in the bark of a tree called Jat'ropha elas'tica, (Monoecia Monadelphia,) and when fresh and pure, is of a whitish colour; but it becomes brown by exposure to the air. The Indians make boots of it, which are water-proof, and when smoaked, look like leather: the inhabitants of Quito, in South-America, prepare from it a kind of cloth which they use as we do oil-cloth and sail-cloth; and in India, flambeaux are made of it, that burn without a wick, and are used by fishermen when they go out at night to fish. A gum of the same kind as Indian rubber is procured from several other trees; among which is the Jaca-tree, that I have already mentioned to you.

The Tallow-tree, Stillin'gia sebif'era, (Monoecia Monadelphia,) is remarkable for the quantity and peculiar nature of the oil obtained from its berries; which so nearly resembles wax or spermaceti, that candles are made of it: but they produce a very disagreeable smell in burning. The tree is a native of China.

Besides these plants, the class Monoecia of Linnæus, contains some of the most valuable trees that grow in England, either natives, or introduced from foreign countries; among which are the oak, the pines, beech, birch, and mulberry; and the genus Cu'cumis, which includes the melon and the common cucumber, with several other species, also belongs to it.

In the twenty-second class, DIOECIA, the stamens and pistils are in different flowers, and on separate plants; the orders in general depend upon the number of stamens.

This class, among other valuable species, contains the great Date-palm, the Pistachia-tree, hemp, and the nutmeg-tree; with several others that I have already mentioned to you, among the native plants.

The genus Sa'lix, or willow, is a very numerous one; containing about sixty native, and several foreign species. On some trees, all the flowers contain stamens only, (two in each flower;) and on others, a pistil only, with a divided summit, and a single seed-vessel close below. The flowers are collected, in both cases, into what are called catkins, from their resemblance to the tail of a cat; each little flower having neither calyx nor petals, but being separated from the rest by a small scale. In the table of the classes, [PLATE 2. Class 22.] you will see two such catkins as I describe, with a flower of each kind magnified.

The Date-palm, Phœnix dactylif'era, is a native of the Levant; and grows from sixty to a hundred feet high, with a cluster of leaves like branches, eight or nine feet long, springing from the top, spreading all round like an umbrella, and bending towards the ground. The shape of the fruit is something like that of an acorn. There is scarcely any part of the date-tree that is not useful: it supplies the place of corn to the inhabitants of the countries where it grows, and furnishes them with almost the whole of their subsistence. Besides the fruit, they eat the young leaves; and of the old ones they make mats, and many other articles, with which they carry on a considerable trade. The tree, when wounded, produces a white juice, called by the natives the milk of the date; which has a sweet and agreeable taste, and is given to invalids as a refreshment: and even the stones of the fruit, though very hard, are not thrown away, for when bruised or softened in water, they are given to sheep and camels as food.

The Pistachia-nut-tree, Pista'cia terebin'thus, (Dioecia Pentandria,) grows naturally in Arabia, Persia, and Syria, from whence the nuts are brought to Europe. I will show you some of them after dinner; they contain a kernel of a pale greenish colour, and of a pleasant flavour.

You have often heard of hemp, Can'nabis sati'va, (Dioecia Pentandria,) which, though cultivated in many parts of England, particularly in Lincolnshire and Suffolk, is a native of India.

EDWARD.

Is it not of hemp that ropes are made?

MOTHER.

It is; and sail-cloth also; and the seeds yield a great quantity of oil. The whole plant, when fresh, has a disagreeable smell, and the water in which the stalks are soaked, for the purpose of separating the tough rind or outer coating, becomes poisonous.

The Nutmeg-tree, Myris'tica moscha'ta, is very beautiful, and grows abundantly in the East-Indies. The leaves have a very fragrant smell, as well as the fruit, which is about the size of a nectarine, and consists of three coats; the first a fleshy pulp; the second a coloured membrane, which is the spice called mace; and the third, a shell containing the nutmeg, which is the seed of the plant. In India, the nutmeg-fruit, preserved entire, is introduced with tea, but the pulp and mace only are eaten.

The plants of the twenty-third class, POLYGAMIA, bear flowers of three different kinds; with stamens, or pistils, or with both; and these grow either on the same plant, or on two, or three distinct ones. But several good botanists think this class unnecessary, as very few plants have these characters. The only species belonging to it, that I recollect, are the Plantain-tree, the Sensitive plant, and the fig.

The first of these, Mu'sa paradisi'aca, is one of the greatest blessings the inhabitants of hot climates enjoy, from the nourishment afforded by its fruit. It is cultivated in all the West-Indian islands, where the plantains serve the negroes instead of bread. The tree rises with a soft stalk fifteen or twenty feet high; and the leaves, which are often eight feet long, come out from the top on every side. The fruit, or plantains, are about a foot long and from three to six inches round; they have a tough skin, and within it a soft pulp of a very sweet flavour, which is roasted and eaten. Every part of the tree is applied to some useful purpose in the West-Indies.

The Sensitive-plant, Mimo'sa pudi'ca, which you have seen in the hot-house, is a native of Brazil; and belongs to a genus, several species of which have the singular property of moving their leaves or branches when touched.

The common fig, Fi'cus car'ica, is a native of the south of Europe. What we consider as the fruit, is called by Linnæus the receptacle, or common calyx, of the flowers; and he describes it as being top-shaped, fleshy, closed at the broad end, with several scales, and having the inside covered with little flowers, both perfect and imperfect, sometimes in the same fruit, and sometimes on different trees. In most plants it is the flower that contains the young fruit; but in this, it is the fruit that encloses and conceals the flower.

It was a long time before it was known how the fig is propagated; and the history of this singular tree is so curious, that at some future time you shall read an account of it.

CONVERSATION THE EIGHTEENTH.

CLASS 24. CRYPTOGAMIA. — ORDERS. — FERNS. — MOSSES; THEIR VARIOUS USES. — LICHENS. — REIN-DEER MOSS, OR LICHEN. — SEA-WEEDS. — MUSHROOMS.

MOTHER.

The plants of the twenty-fourth class, Cryptogamia, are so very different from those of all the other classes, that the study of them may be considered as forming a distinct department of botany; and I do not recommend them to your particular attention, unless hereafter you wish to devote a large portion of your time to this subject. There are several books well calculat to assist your progress, whenever you are disposed to pursue it; and you will be equally astonished and pleased, at the wonderful regularity and minuteness of the parts of these plants, and the beautiful contrivances of nature for their nourishment and distribution.

I have already told you, that the character of this class consists, in the plants that compose it

Fern

Moſs

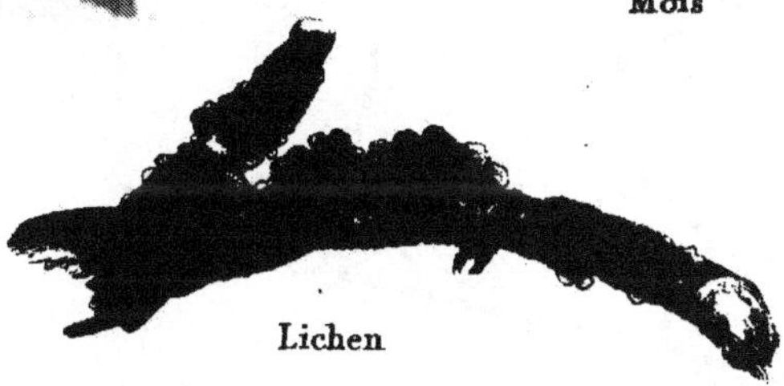

Lichen

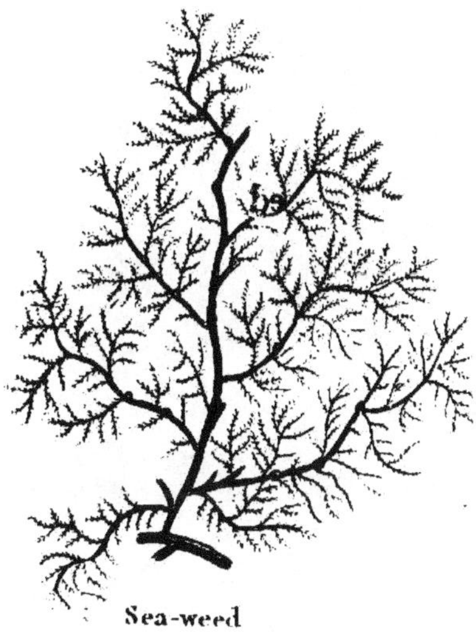

Sea-weed

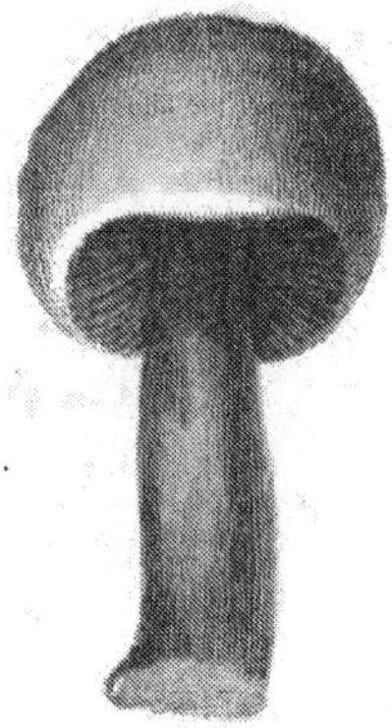

Mushroom

Class XXIV. *CRYPTOGAMIA*.

having flowers, in which the stamens and pistils are either not well ascertained, or not to be numbered with certainty; so that they cannot be referred to any of the preceding classes.*

The orders into which the class is now divided, are five; consisting of tribes quite different from each other in their characters.

The first is called Fil'ices, or ferns; the second, Mus'ci, or mosses, includes a great many genera and species; the third, Hepat'icae, or liverworts, consists of genera, bearing some resemblance to the mosses; the fourth, called Algae, comprehends the lichens, and sea-weeds; and the fifth, Fungi, contains all the mushrooms and funguses. Withering, and some other botanists, have another order besides, which they call miscellaneous, including plants that are not easily referred to any of the tribes I have just mentioned. The drawing that I have made for you, [see Plate 20.] is intended merely to show the general appearance of some of the most common cryptogamic genera.

The Ferns, in general, have what is called their fruit disposed in spots or lines upon the under side of the leaves; and the genera are distinguished, principally, by the shape and structure of these spots. They are a beautiful tribe;

* Smith's Introduction, &c. p. 302.

but the uses to which they are applied are not very numerous.

Several of our common kinds of ferns are employed as firing by the poorer classes of people; who also mix the ashes with water, and form them into balls, which they dry in the sun, and use in-instead of soap for washing their linen.

The leaves of most of the species, if cut when fully grown and properly dried, make a thatch for houses more durable than any sort of straw; and the root of one kind, called royal moonwort, Osmun'da rega'lis, when boiled in water, is employed in the north of Europe, like starch, to stiffen linen.

In South America, some of the ferns, not unlike our common brakes or polypody, Pte'ris Aquili'na, grow to such a size, that they may be compared to trees. There is one species found in North America, called the sensitive fern, Onoc'lea sensib'ilis, which is remarkable for withering soon after it is touched by the human hand, but endures the touch of other bodies without being at all injured. Sprengel, a German botanist, who wished to prove the truth of this curious circumstance, repeated the experiment several times, and always with the same effect.

The Mosses, which form the second order of this class, have roots and leaves something like those of other plants; but the fruit is very different. Small threads, like the filaments of stamens, generally grow out of the bosom of the leaves, and support little roundish bodies, that resemble anthers, but which are really the capsules that contain the seeds: These capsules are hollow, of various figures, and in general furnished with what is called a calyptra, or veil, like a little extinguisher: and when this is removed, the mouth of the capsule itself, which sometimes has a lid besides, is found to be surrounded with one or two rows of fringe of great delicacy, and of surprising regularity in the number of the teeth that compose it. The genera of mosses, are founded chiefly upon the situation of the capsule, with some other circumstances; among which the structure of the fringe at the mouth is the most important.

The mosses are generally perennial and evergreen, and capable of growing in much colder climates and situations than most other vegetables. I have heard, that in Spitzbergen the rocks which rise there out of everlasting masses of ice, are thickly clothed with mosses; and a botanist, named Crantz, who travelled in Greenland, counted above twenty different species, without moving from a rock where he was seated.

Mosses possess the singular property of reviving when moistened, after having become very dry and to all appearance withered; and even after they have been gathered and kept in a dry state for many years, if put into water, every part of them will expand, and become apparently as fresh and green as when they were growing. They overspread the trunks and roots of trees, and in winter defend them against frost; in wet weather they preserve them from decay, and, during the greatest drought, provide them with moisture, and protect them from the burning heat of the sun.

The poor Laplanders derive several of their comforts from the mosses. Of the golden maiden-hair, Polyt'richum commu'ne, (one of the largest species belonging to this tribe,) they form excellent beds, by cutting thick layers of it, one of which serves as a mattrass, and the other as a coverlet: and Linnæus tells us, that he himself often made use of such a bed, when he was travelling in Lapland. These mossy cushions are very elastic; so that a bed may be rolled up into a parcel small enough to be carried under a man's arm, and the inhabitants can easily take them about with them in their journies. They do not grow hard by pressure; and when they lose a part of their elasticity by long use, it can soon be restored by dipping them in water.

The Lapland women make great use of the gray bog-moss, Sphag'num palus'tre, which is particularly soft. They wrap their infants up in it without any other clothing, and place them in leathern cradles, lined with the moss; and in these soft and warm nests the little babies are completely defended from the cold.

There is a plant of another genus in this class, Lycopo'dium clava'tum; which, though not belonging to the same order, is called club-moss, the seeds of which are collected and sold in various parts of Europe, for the purpose of producing the appearance of lightning on the stage at theatres; for being very light and combustible, they take fire with a sort of hissing noise while floating in the air.

The structure of the mosses is so beautiful, that they are objects of the greatest interest and admiration, to all who understand them. Mungo Park, a traveller celebrated for his fortitude and courage, who ventured alone into the midst of the great unknown countries of Africa, wrote an account of his journey, that will give you pleasure at some future time; and I will now read you a part of it.—"I saw myself in the midst of a vast wilderness, naked and alone, surrounded by savage animals, and by men still more savage. I was five hundred miles from the nearest European settlement; I considered my fate as certain, and that I had no alternative but to lie down and perish. At this moment, the extraordinary beauty of a small moss irresistibly caught my eye; and though the whole plant was not larger than the top of one of my fingers, I could not contemplate the delicate conformation of its roots, leaves, and capsules, without admiration. Can that being, thought I, who planted, watered, and brought to perfection, in this obscure part of the world, a thing which appears of so small importance, look with unconcern upon the situation and sufferings of creatures formed after his own image?—Reflections like these would not allow me to despair: I started up, and disregarding both hunger and fatigue, travelled forwards, assured that relief was at hand; and I was not disappointed."

EDWARD.

And did he ever come home?

MOTHER.

He did, my dear; but he went out again to Africa, to make new discoveries, and was killed by some of the natives.

The HEPAT'ICÆ, or Liverworts, form the next order of cryptogamic plants; but I shall not dwell upon them at present.

The ALGÆ consist of plants, some of which are formed of a mere crust, others of a leathery or jelly-like substance;—and there are two principal divisions; the Lichens,—and the Aquatic, or Submersed Algæ, some of which abound in fresh water, others in the sea. The latter are commonly called sea-weeds; and the genera, in both divisions of the order, are distinguished, either by the situation of what is supposed to be the flower or seed, or by the resemblance of the whole plant to some other well-known substance.

The Li'chens commonly grow in fleshy or leather-like patches, on the stems of trees, rocks, old buildings, palings, and other solid bodies.

EDWARD.

Are those lichens, that grow like rough yellow and bluish crusts, upon the old gooseberry-bushes and apple-trees in the garden? I think your drawing is like them.

MOTHER.

They are some of the most common species.—The lichens, as well as the mosses, are found to thrive in all kinds of soil, and in every climate: and, like the mosses, they have the property of growing again, when placed in situations adapted to them, though they may have been kept in a dry state for many years. They are not destroyed either by heat or severe cold, and are found growing where no other vegetation is to be seen.

One species of this tribe of plants, the Li'chen rangiferi'nus, or rein-deer moss, is the most useful vegetable that grows throughout the whole of

Lapland; for it is the principal food of the rein-deer, without which valuable creature the inhabitants of that miserable country could scarcely exist. The rein-deer draws them in sledges, over countries buried in snow; its flesh and milk afford them nourishment, its skin cloathing, and even its bones and sinews are made into several useful articles.

The rein-deer lichen, or moss, (as it is sometimes called,) is of a whitish colour, and grows in Lapland to the height of at least a foot, covering the ground like snow; but in this country, where it is found in some mountainous situations, it seldom attains the height of six inches.

The inhabitants of Iceland find another species of lichen, called Iceland-moss, (Li'chen Islandicus,) which grows abundantly in that country, highly serviceable; they make use of it as food in various ways, and consider it as very nourishing.

Several different species of lichen afford beautiful dyes; and one of them, called dyers'-lichen or orchall, Li'chen roccel'la, is particularly valuable, from its communicating to wool and silk various shades of purple and crimson. This plant, which is brought chiefly from the Archipelago and the Canary islands, is of great importance as an article of commerce; and when scarce, has been sold for even a thousand pounds a ton.

The purple powder, called Cudbear, that is used

in dying purple, is prepared from the Li'chen tartar'eus, which is common in many parts of England; but it can be used only for dying woollen cloth, as it does not communicate its colour to vegetable substances.

The aquatic Algæ, including the sea-weeds, imbibe all their nourishment through their surface, the roots serving only to fasten them to the bottom; and many of them float about in the water, without being attached to any solid body. They constitute a very large tribe.

Of the Sea-weeds, some are used as food, and all are of great importance to the farmers on the sea-coast, for manuring their land. In the islands of Jura and Skye, the bladder-fucus, or sea-wrack, Fu'cus vesiculo'sus, often serves as winter-food for the cattle, which regularly go down to the shores, when the tide is out, to eat it; and even the deer have been observed to come from the mountains to feed upon this plant. Linnæus says, that the inhabitants of Gothland, in Sweden, boil this fucus in water, and feed their hogs with it, mixed with meal: in Scandinavia, the poor people thatch their cottages with it. But one of the most important purposes to which this sea-weed is applied, in common with many other species, is the preparation of kelp, which is a principal ingredient in the manufacture of soap.

If the leaves of this plant receive a wound, while growing, abundance of young shoots are thrown out from the injured part; and even if a hole or rent be made in the middle of a leaf, a new one will spring from each side of it.

In Scotland, the sea-tangle, Fu'cus digita'tus, as well as the dulse, Fu'cus palma'tus, is employed as food; and the stems of the former plant are sometimes used for making handles of knives. For this purpose a thick stem is chosen, and cut into pieces about four inches long; the hilts of the knives are stuck into these, while fresh, and, as the stem dries, it contracts and hardens firmly around them. These handles, when tipped with metal, can scarcely be distinguished from horn. The large stalks of the plant are dried, and used as fuel in the Orkney and Shetland islands.

The size that some of the larger kinds of sea-weeds attain, and the rapidity of their growth, are truly wonderful. The gigantic fucus, Fu'cus gigante'us, is said to extend often to the length of a thousand or fifteen hundred feet: and it grows in such profusion, that the masses of it resemble islands. In the Atlantic, Pacific, and Indian Oceans, there are vast tracts of sea-weeds; one of which has been called by navigators the grassy sea, from its great extent: The entire surface in such places is literally covered with these plants; and ships on their voyages are several days in passing through them.

The Fu'cus te'nax is employed in China as glue and gum-arabic are with us: when washed and steeped in warm water, it dissolves, and as it cools stiffens into a glue, with which large sheets of paper are coated, in order to make them transparent; and these are used, instead of glass, for lanterns and windows. In China, too, windows are sometimes made of slips of bamboo, which are crossed, and the spaces between filled up with thin sheets of this glue alone.

The Fu'cus lichenöi'des is in high estimation in the East Indies, particularly at Ceylon, as a luxury for the table. You will be surprised to hear that the nests of a kind of swallow are eaten as a delicacy, in China, and throughout the east, and even imported to London. These nests, it is supposed are made by the birds almost entirely of the Fu'cus lichenöi'des.

The little branch of sea-weed that I have sketched for you, [PLATE 20.] does not resemble any of the kinds which I have been speaking of: It is a species of the genus Conferva; and I have drawn it, merely to give you an idea of the difference between the aquatic algæ and the lichens, which form the two divisions of the order Algæ. Several species of conferva are found to be very beautiful and curious, when examined with a magnifying glass.

The FUNGI are a very singular tribe: they have, properly, no leaves; their whole substance being fleshy, generally of quick growth and short duration, and differing in firmness, from a watery pulp to a leathery or even woody texture. Several of the species are poisonous.

The only kind of fungus that we venture to eat, is the Agar'icus campes'tris, or common mushroom; which is often cultivated in hot-beds, and grows wild in parks and fields, that have been undisturbed by ploughing for many years together. The most splendid of all the mushrooms, Agar'icus xerampeli'nus, is common in Italy, and is brought to the markets there for sale as food; but it is very rarely found in England. It is of a beautiful red and orange colour. But the Agar'icus delicio'sus, which also grows in Italy, and has been found in England, is of much superior flavour, and was highly prized as a luxury by the ancient Romans.

In Lapland, Linnæus saw the Bole'tus ignia'rius, another kind of mushroom, which is shaped like a horse's hoof, hung up on the walls of the cottages, and used as a pincushion. It is made use of also as tinder, in some parts of England and Germany.

I have now told you, my dear Edward, all that I intended to mention about Botany: and I hope that what you have already learned will enable you to make use of books, upon this interesting subject, without my assistance. I shall be very much gratified, if your desire to pursue it is at all increased by any thing that I have said.

EXPLANATION

OF

THE BOTANICAL TERMS

MADE USE OF IN THIS VOLUME.

*** Some of the terms in this list are accented, and are to be pronounced, in the same manner as the Latin names of Plants, in the preceding part of the Volume.

A

Alternate, branches, leaves or flowers;—coming out regularly one above another, but on different sides; not opposite.

Angiospermia; the name of one of the orders of the class Didynamia; in which the seeds are enclosed in a seed-vessel.

Annual, plants or roots; living only one year.

Anther; the uppermost part of a *Stamen*, fixed upon the top of the *Filament*, and containing the *Pollen*.

Arrow-shaped; like the head of an arrow; as the leaves of common sorrel, or the anther of the crocus. (Plate 4.)

AWL-SHAPED; slender, and becoming finer towards the end, like an awl; as the filaments of the flowering rush. (Plate 9.)

AWN; a slender, stiff, sharp substance, growing from the husks of some grasses and other flowers; as in oats, barley, and the teasel.

B

BARK; the outermost covering of the roots, stems, and branches of vegetables. It is generally divided into three parts; the cuticle or skin, the outer, and the inner bark.

BERRY; a pulpy seed-vessel, without valves; in which the seeds are surrounded with the pulp: as in the gooseberry, and the common holly. (Plate 5.)

BIENNIAL; living two years, and then perishing. In biennial plants, a root and leaves are formed during the first year, and the flower and fruit completed in the second.

BLOSSOM, (Corolla); that part of a flower which is generally coloured, and consists of one or more petals. (Plate 1.)

BORDER; the upper spreading part of a blossom of one petal: as in the germander-speedwell. (Plate 3.)

BRISTLES; strong, stiff, roundish hairs.

BULB; } BULBOUS-ROOT; } the part commonly round and fleshy, from which the stem of some plants arises, and which sends down fibres into the ground. A bulbous-root is either *solid*, as in the crocus and snow-drop, (Plates 4 and 7.) — *coated*, as in the onion, — or *scaly*, as in the lily.

Bulging; swelling out irregularly; as the two outer leaves in the calyx of the wall-flower. (Plates 1 and 15.)

Bunch; a fruit-stalk, or flower-stalk, furnished with short branches at the sides. The white and red currants grow in bunches; as also the flowers of germander-speedwell. (Plate 3.)

C

Calyx; that part of a flower which, in general, grows close under the corolla. There are seven different kinds of calyx; but the following only are mentioned in this volume, viz.

A *cup*, as in the corn-cockle and ground-ivy. (Plates 10 and 14.)

An *involucrum*, as in the flowering-rush. (Plate 9.)

A *catkin*, as in the willow. (Plate 2. Class Dioecia.)

A *sheath*, as in the crocus and snow-drop. (Plates 4 and 7.)

A *veil*, as in the mosses. (Plate 20.)

Capsule; a dry hollow seed vessel, which opens naturally, when the seeds are ripe, to let them out; as in the poppy. (Plate 13.)

CATKIN; a composition of flowers and chaff, upon a long, slender, thread-shaped receptacle; the whole resembling the tail of a cat: as in the common willow. (Plate 2. Class Dioecia.)

CELL; a hollow space in a seed-vessel (particularly in a capsule), for holding the seed. (Page 113.)

CENTRE-FLORETS; those which occupy the middle part of a compound flower; as the yellow ones in the daisy. (Plate 19.) — See FLORET.

CIRCUMFERENCE; the outward line or boundary of a circle. The word is used, in speaking of compound flowers, to express the florets that are farthest from the centre; as the white ones, which surround the yellow, in the daisy. (Plate 19.)

CLAW; the lower part of the petal, which stands within the calyx, in a polypetalous flower; as in the wall-flower. (Plate 1.)

CLIMBERS; plants which are weak, and require the support of some other body to raise themselves upon; as the ivy and vine. The climbers *do not twine* round the bodies to which they are attached. (See p. 72.)

CLOVEN; divided or split, the edges of the divisions being straight; as the summit of the pistil in ground-ivy. (Plate 14.) — See NOTCHED.

COATED; composed of layers, one over another; like an onion.

COLOURED; of any other colour than green. The calyx is sometimes coloured.

COMMON; applied to the *Calyx*; — containing several blossoms; as in plants of the class Syngenesia, dandelion, thistle, daisy, &c. (Plate 19.)

COMPOUND; a term applied to the flowers of the class Syngenesia, which consist of many florets, or little flowers, placed upon one receptacle, and included within one common calyx: as the daisy. (Plate 19.)

COMPRESSED; flattened on the sides.

CONE; a solid body shaped like a sugar-loaf. — The fruit of the fir, and of several other trees, is called a cone, because it has this shape.

CONICAL; shaped like a cone or sugar-loaf; as the receptacle of the daisy. (Plate 19.)

CREEPING; extending itself along or under the ground, and putting forth roots or fibres; applied to stems and roots.

CROSS-SHAPED-FLOWERS, are those, which have four equal petals, spreading out in the form of a cross; as the wall-flower. (Plates 1 and 15.)

CRUCIFORM; cross-shaped.

CRYPTOGAMIA; the name given by Linnæus to the *twenty-fourth Class:* stamens and pistils not visible to the naked eye, or not ascertained. (Plates 2, and 20.)

CUP; a kind of calyx, so called because it is commonly shaped like a cup. It is either of one leaf, as in mouse ear and corn-cockle, (Plates 6 and 10.); or formed of several leaves, as in wall-flower (Plates 1 and 15): and is sometimes double, as in mallow. (Plate 16.) And it contains either one flower, as in the examples above-mentioned, or several, as in the daisy. (Plate 19.)

D

DECANDRIA; the name of the *tenth Class;* ten stamens in each flower. (Plates 2 and 10.)

DECUMBENT; (applied to the stalk), lying upon the ground, or near it.

DIADELPHIA; the name of the *seventeenth Class;* filaments united in two sets; flowers butterfly-shaped. (Plates 2 and 17.)

DIANDRIA; the name of the *second Class;* two stamens in each flower; as germander speedwell. (Plates 2 and 3.) — Also the name of an *Order*, in the classes Gynandria, Monoecia, and Dioecia.

DIDYNAMIA; the name of the *fourteenth Class;* four stamens in each flower, two of them long, and two short. (Plates 2 and 14.)

DIGYN'IA; the name of one of the orders in each of the first thirteen classes, except the ninth and twelfth; — two pistils in each flower.

DIOECIA; the name of the *twenty-second Class;* the flowers containing stamens growing on distinct plants from those with pistils. (See Plate 2.) — Also the name of one of the *Orders* in the class Polygamia.

DODECAGYNIA; the name of one of the orders in the eleventh Class; twelve to eighteen or twenty pistils in each flower.

DODECANDRIA; the name of the *eleventh Class;* from eleven to nineteen stamens in each flower. (Plates 2 and 11.)

DOUBLE-CALYX; one calyx within another, as in the mallow. (Plate 16.)

DOUBLE; a flower is commonly so called, when the petals exceed the usual number, while some of the stamens remain. (page 91.) See FULL.

DOWN; the fine hair, or feather-like substance, with which the seeds of some plants are furnished; as in the dandelion and several other compound flowers. (See page 162.)

E

ENNEANDRIA; the name of the *ninth Class*; nine stamens in each flower. (Plates 2 and 9.) — And also of one of the *Orders* in the classes Monadelphia and Dioecia.

EVERGREEN; bearing green leaves throughout all seasons of the year; as the common holly. (See p. 40.)

F

FARINA; the pollen.

FEATHERED; applied to hair, bristles, or down; having smaller hairs growing on the sides. The down of seeds sometimes consists of simple hairs; sometimes it is feathered, — as in dandelion. (See page 162.)

FERNS (Fil'ices); the name of a natural tribe of plants,

which form one of the orders of the class Cryptogamia. (Plates 2 and 20.)

FILAMENT; that part of a *stamen* which supports the *anther*. (Plate 1.)

FIL'ICES; ferns.

FLESHY; of a consistence more solid than pulp; as the fruit of the apple, the root of the turnip, and the leaves of some plants. The soft part of a cherry or gooseberry, is called *pulpy*.

FLORET; a little flower. One of those which constitute a compound flower: as in the daisy. (Plate 19.)

FLOWER; that part of a plant which produces the seed.

FRUIT; the seed or seeds, with their seed-vessel;—but the seed is the essential part.

FRUIT-STALK; a stem or branch bearing fruit or flowers, but not leaves. (See Plates 3, 9, &c.)

FULL; this term is applied to the flowers commonly called *double*, when by richness of soil, or other causes, *all the stamens* have been changed into petals. Full flowers cannot produce seeds. (See page 91.)

FUNGI, (fungusses, mushrooms); the name of one of the orders in the class Cryptogamia. (Plate 20.)

FUNNEL-SHAPED; applied to a blossom of one petal, with the lower part like a tube, and the upper like a cup; as in the mezereon. (Plate 8.)

G.

GAPING; a term applied to the blossoms of several plants, in the class Didynamia, from their resemblance to an open mouth: as ground-ivy. (Plate 14.)

Gelatinous; like jelly.

Genus; one of the subdivisions in the systematical arrangement of plants; containing those, of the same classes and orders, which agree in their flowers and fruit. (See page 16.)

Germen; the lower part of a pistil.—It is the young fruit, scarcely formed; and becomes afterwards a seed-vessel, (capsule, pod, or legumen, &c.) (See Plate 1.)—The germen is sometimes placed below the calyx and corolla, sometimes within them.

Glands; solid bodies, which afford a peculiar fluid, differently situated in different plants: as in the wall-flower, where they are placed at the foot of the shorter stamens. (Plate 1.)

Gramina; } a natural family of plants; comprehend-
Grasses; } ing those in the order Digynia, of the class Triandria. (See Page 32, and 127.)

Grinning; see Ringent.

Gymnospermia; the name of one of the orders of the class Didynamia; in which the seeds have no covering: as in the ground-ivy. (Plate 14.)

Gynandria; the name of the *twentieth Class;* stamens growing upon the pistils. The flowers of this class have a very peculiar structure; as in the Orchises. (Plate 2.)

H

Heads *of Flowers;* when several flowers grow thickly together, in a kind of ball, they are said to form

Heads; as in the common red and white clover, and the lotus. (Plate 17.)

HEART-SHAPED; a term applied to some leaves and petals, from their resemblance to the shape of a heart. When the narrow end is next the stem, the term is *inversely heart-shaped*; as the petals of the Mallow. (Plate 16.)

HEPTAGYNIA; the name of one of the orders in the seventh class.

HEPTANDRIA; the name of the *seventh Class;* seven stamens in each flower. (See Plate 2.)

HERB; or HERBACEOUS PLANT, (opposed to *woody;*) terms applied to plants that are succulent and tender. The mouse-ear, and common garden-pea, are *herbs;* the stem of the wall-flower is somewhat *woody;* the mezereon is a *shrub;* the ash, oak, &c. are *trees.*

HEXAGYNIA; the name of one of the orders in the sixth, ninth, and thirteenth classes; in which each flower has six pistils; as in the flowering-rush. (Plate 9.)

HEXANDRIA; the name of the *sixth Class;* six stamens in each flower. (Plates 2 and 7.)

HUSK; the calyx and blossom of the grasses are called husks: they are thin and dry, like chaff; consisting of one or more leaves, called valves, with or without awns; and containing the grain or seed.

I

ICOSANDRIA; the name of the *twelfth Class;* twenty

stamens or more, *fixed to the calyx.* (Plates 2 and 12.)

IMPERFECT FLOWER; wanting either stamens, or pistils, or both; as in the classes Monoecia and Dioecia. (Plate 2.) The florets of the border in the daisy, are imperfect; having no stamens. (Plate 19.) — A flower that wants the calyx, or corolla, is not called *imperfect*, but *incomplete*; as the mezereon. (Plate 8.) (See p. 78.)

INFERIOR; applied, principally, to the *germen*, when it is placed *below the cup*; as in the snowdrop. (Plate 7.)

INVOLU'CRUM; a sort of calyx distant from the corolla; exemplified principally, but not exclusively, in umbelliferous plants. The calyx in the flowering rush, (Plate 9.) is an involucrum.

J

JOINTED-STEM; one that has knots, or joints, like the straw of wheat, &c.

K

KEEL; the lowermost petal in a butterfly-shaped blossom, so called from its resemblance to the keel of a boat. (See Plate 17.)

KNOTS; the joints of the stem, of grasses and reeds.

L

LABIATE, or lipped; applied to a corolla of an irregular figure, with two lips; as in several flowers of the class Didynamia. (See Plate 14.)

LEAFIT, or LEAFLET; one of the smaller leaves, in a leaf composed of many; as in the dog-rose. (Plate 12.)

LEAF-STALK; the stalk which supports a leaf, but not a flower.

LEGUMEN; a seed-vessel of two valves, in which the seeds are fixed to one seam only; as in the common pea, (see page 149.)

LEGUMINOUS PLANTS; those in which the seed-vessel is a legumen; as the lotus. (Plate 17.)

LID; the cover of the capsule in several of the mosses.

LIPS; the upper and under divisions of a labiate or gaping-blossom. (Plate 14.)

M

MONADELPHIA; the name of the *sixteenth Class*; all the filaments united in a tube round the pistil. (Plates 2. and 16.)

MONANDRIA; the name of the *first Class*; one stamen in each flower. (Plate 2.)

MONOECIA; the name of the *twenty-first Class*; stamens and pistils in separate flowers, but on the same plant. (Plate 2.)—Also the name of one of the *Orders* in the *twenty-third Class*, Polygamia, of Linnæus.

MONOGYNIA; the name of the first order in each of the first thirteen classes; one pistil in each flower.

MONOPETALOUS; a blossom is so called, when it is composed of only one petal; as in Veronica (Plate 3.); Crocus (Plate 4.); Daphne (Plate 8.); Glechoma, (Plate 14.)

MOSSES, (Musci); a natural tribe of plants, forming one of the orders in the class Cryptogamia.

MOUTH; the opening of the *tube*, in blossoms composed of one petal; as in mouse-ear (Plate 6.); and Ground-ivy. (Plate 14.)

MUSCI, Mosses.

MUSHROOMS, (Fungi.) The name of a natural tribe of plants, forming one of the orders in the class Cryptogamia. (Plate 20.)

N

NAMES. The botanical names of plants, are, in every case, two;—the *generic*, which applies to all those of the same genus; and what is called the *trivial* name, which is confined to those of one species only. Whenever a third name occurs, it denotes *a variety*. —Thus, Geranium-malvifolium-pusillum signifies a very small variety of the Geranium-malvifolium, or mallow-leaved Geranium.

NATURAL order or class; an assemblage of several Genera of plants, which agree in their general appearance, and qualities; as the umbelliferous, and leguminous tribes, the grasses, &c.

NECTARY; a part of a flower, in which honey is supposed to be formed or contained; of various forms in different flowers. (See pages 7, and 66.)

NODDING; a term applied to a flower, when its stalk is bent down near the end; as in the daffodil and hyacinth.

NOTCHED, at the end or sides; having angular incisions not so deep as when *cloven*; like the summits of the pistils in the flowering rush. (Plate 9.)

NUT; a seed inclosed by a hard woody shell: as the common hazel nut; and the kernel or stone of the peach, plum, and cherry, &c.

O

OCTANDRIA; the name of the *eighth Class*; eight stamens in each flower. (Plates 2, and 8.)

OPPOSITE; leaves or branches, growing in pairs from the same part of the stem, but on opposite sides; as in the germander-speedwell. (Plate 3.)

P

PAPILIONACEOUS; butterfly-shaped: — some blossoms are so called from their resemblance to a butterfly, in Latin *Papilio*. The term is applied to plants of the class Diadelphia. (Plates 2 and 17.)

PARASITICAL; growing upon some other plant, not in the ground; as the miseltoe. (See page 45.)

PENTAGYNIA; the name of one of the orders in the fifth, tenth, eleventh, twelfth, and thirteenth classes; five pistils in each flower.

Pentandria; the name of the *fifth Class;* five stamens in each flower. (Plates 2, and 6.)

Perennial; lasting for many years, or at least more than two.

Perfect Flower; having both stamens and pistils. — See Imperfect.

Permanent; applied principally to the calyx: — remaining on the plant after the fruit is ripe; as in the mouse ear (Plate 6.) and ground ivy (Plate 14.)

Petals; the leaves which constitute the blossom, or corolla, of a flower. They are generally coloured. (Plate 1.)

Pillar; a little shaft, or stem, supporting part of the down of some seeds; as in dandelion, (see page 162.) The term is applied also to the receptacle, around which the capsules are placed, in the Mallow (Plate 16.)

Pistil; part of a flower, composed of the *germen*, *style*, and *summit*. (Plate 1.)

Pod; a seed-vessel, composed of two valves or shells; with a partition, upon which the seeds are placed, being fixed, alternately, to each of the seams or sides. (See Plate 15, and page 149.)

Pollen, or Farina; a fine powder contained in the anthers of flowers.

Polyadelphia; the name of the *eighteenth Class;* stamens united, by the filaments, in three or more sets. (Plates 2, and 18.)

Polyandria; the name of the *thirteenth Class;* more than twenty stamens, *fixed to the receptacle.* (Plates 2, and 13.)

Polygamia; the name of the *twenty-third Class* of Linnæus; three different sorts of flowers, on the same, or on separate plants; some of them containing pistils, some stamens, and others both. (See Plate 2.) The term is applied also to each of the *Orders* of the class Syngenesia; and signifies that several florets are enclosed within one common calyx: the five orders being named as follows, viz.

Polygamia equalis; all the flowers furnished with both stamens and pistils.

——— *superflua;* florets of the centre, having both stamens and pistils, those of the circumference pistils only. The common daisy, (Plate 19.) is an example of this order.

——— *frustranea;* florets of the centre having both stamens and pistils, those of the circumference neither.

——— *necessaria;* florets of the centre having stamens and pistils, without seeds; those of the circumference pistils only, with seeds.

——— *segregata;* several florets enclosed within one common calyx; each having, besides, a separate cup of its own.

Polygynia; the name of one of the orders, in the fifth, sixth, twelfth, and thirteenth classes.

Polypetalous; corolla, or flower; having more than one petal: as the rose, or the poppy. (Plates 12 and 13.)

Prickles; sharp points growing from the *bark* only f a plant, and coming off along with it: as in the rose, (Plate 12.) and bramble. *Thorns* grow from the *wood*.

PROCUMBENT; lying on the ground; but without putting forth roots.

PULPY; softer than fleshy; applied to fruit, as in the gooseberry and currant, and sometimes to leaves. A cherry is pulpy, but an apple is fleshy

R

RECEPTACLE; the seat or base, upon which all the other parts of a flower are placed, and by which they are connected. It is remarkable in the artichoke, but in some flowers is not conspicuous. (See Plate 1, and page 7.)

RINGENT, or grinning; a term applied to the corolla of several flowers of the class Didynamia in which the border is divided into two parts, called lips, and is supposed to resemble an *open* mouth: — as in ground ivy, (Plate 14.) When the lips are closed, the flower is called *Personate*.

ROOT; that part of a plant which grows in the earth and supplies the rest with nourishment. It may be fibrous, bulbous, or tuberous as in the Potatoe.

S

SAP; the juice of plants.

SCALY; composed of scales lying one over another, like the skin of a fish: as the bulb of a lily, the cup of a thistle, &c.

SEAM; the line formed by the meeting of the valves in

a seed-vessel. The legumen of a pea, is of two valves; and all the seeds are fastened to one of the seams. (See p. 149.)

SEED-VESSEL; a vessel or case containing the seeds. Seed-vessels are of the following kinds, viz.:

A *Capsule;* as in the poppy. (Plate 13.)

A *Pod;* as in the wall-flower. (Plate 1, and p. 149.)

A *Legumen;* as in the lotus. (Plate 17, and p. 149.)

A *Berry;* as in the holly, (Plate 5.) and rose. (Plate 12.)

A *Cone;* as in the fir.

A *Drupa,* inclosing a nut; as in the cherry and peach.

A *Pomum;* as in the apple.

SEGMENTS; the divisions of leaves, cups, or blossoms, &c.

SESSILE. See SITTING.

SHEATH; a kind of calyx; composed of a thin skinny leaf: as in the crocus and snowdrop. (Plates 4, and 7.)

SHRUB; a term commonly applied to plants with a perennial woody stem, divided near the ground into branches. Mezereon is a shrub.

SILICULA; a short broad Pod.

SILICULOSA; the name of one of the orders of the class Tetradynamia; in which the seed-vessels are Siliculas.

SILIQUA; a long narrow pod.

SILIQUOSA; the name of one of the orders of the class Tetradynamia; in which seed-vessels are Siliquas. (Plates 1 and 15.)

SIMPLE; applied to the stem or stalk, means *undivided.*

SITTING, or *Sessile,* leaves or flowers, are joined immediately to the stem ; without leaf-stalks or fruit-stalks : as the leaves of the germander speedwell (Plate 3,) and the flowers of the mezereon (Plate 8.) The term is applied also to the Down of seeds, when there is no *Pillar*, or stalk, between it and the seed. (See p. 162.)

SKINNY ; like skin, or gold-beaters'-leaf ; thin, tough, and transparent.

SOLITARY ; — flowers, seeds, or leaves, are so called, when only one grows upon the same part of a plant.

SPEAR-SHAPED ; shaped like the head of a spear : as the leaves of the mouse-ear. (Plate 6.)

SPECIES ; a set of plants, which agree in the general structure of their flowers and fruit, and therefore belong to the *same Genus*, but differ in their stem, leaves, and other particulars. (See p. 16.)

SPIKE ; a number of *sessile* flowers, placed alternately on each side of a simple flower stalk ; as in many of the grasses.

STAMEN ; part of a flower, composed of a *filament*, and *anther*. (Plate 1.)

STANDARD ; the upper petal of a butterfly-shaped blossom ; as in the lotus, (Plate 17.) The standard is very remarkable in the common pea.

STEM ; the trunk of a plant, supporting the leaves, branches, and flower-stalks, or flowers ; it rises immediately from the root or bulb.

STRAW ; the stem of a grass.

STYLE ; that part of a *Pistil* which stands upon the *germen*, and supports the *summit*.

SUCKERS; shoots, which spring from the root, spread along or under the ground, and then take root themselves.

SUMMIT; the uppermost part of a *pistil.*

SUPERIOR, a term applied to the *calyx* or *corolla,* when it is placed above the germen; which last is then called *inferior:* — as in the snowdrop (Plate 7.) The *germen* is superior, when it is placed above, or within, the calyx or corolla: as in the speedwell, mezereon, and corn-cockle. (Plates 3, 8, and 10.)

SYNGENESIA; the name of the *nineteenth Class;* anthers united, flowers compound. (Plates 2, and 19.)

T

TARGET-SHAPED; round and flattened, something like the under side of a saucer, or the head of a common brass nail: as the summit of the pistil in the poppy. (Plate 13.)

TETRADYNAMIA; the name of the *fifteenth Class;* six stamens in each flower, four long and two short. (Plates 1, and 15.)

TETRAGYNIA; the name of one of the orders, in several of the classes; four pistils in each flower.

TETRANDRIA; the name of the *fourth Class;* four stamens in each flower. (Plates 2, and 5.)

THORNS; sharp-pointed projections, growing *from the woody substance* of a plant: as in the furze, and blackthorn. *Prickles* grow from the *bark* only.

TREE; a vegetable with a single woody trunk, divided at the top into branches, and enduring for many years.

TRIANDRIA; the name of the *third Class;* three stamens in each flower. (Plates 2, and 4.)

TRIGYNIA; the name of one of the orders in several of the classes; three pistils in each flower.

TRIVIAL NAME; that which is added to the generic name, to denote the *species;* as in the *Crocus vernus:* — the first is the generic, the second the trivial name.

TUBE; the lower narrow part of a blossom of one petal, by which it is fixed to the receptacle; as in the crocus, (Plate 4), mezereon, (Plate 8) ground-ivy (Plate 14.)

U

UMBEL; a composition of flowers, in which a number of slender fruit-stalks grow from the same centre, and rise nearly to the same height; so as to form a flat surface at top; as in hemlock, and cow-parsnip: the separate stalks, or ribs, are often called *spokes of the umbel.* (p. 57.)

UMBELLIFEROUS; a term applied to plants, which produce their flowers in umbels.

UMBELLULE; a little umbel. In several umbelliferous plants, each *spoke of the umbel* has an umbellule at its end.

V

Valves; the pieces that compose a seed-vessel. (see the figures at p. 149.) The pod of the wall-flower, (Plate 1,) has two valves, with a partition between them. The term is applied also, to the projecting substances, which close the mouth of the tube, in some blossoms; as in the mouse-ear. (Plate 6.)

Varieties; plants of the *same Species*, which differ slightly from each other; as in colour, size, or some other unimportant circumstance. The purple, yellow, and white crocuses, for example, are varieties of the species vernus. Species can be reproduced from the seeds; but *not varieties*.

Veil; a conical covering of the capsule in several mosses; somewhat like an extinguisher. (Plates 2, and 20.)

W

Wheel-shaped; a term applied to a blossom of one petal, with a flat border, and a very short tube; like that of the germander speedwell. (Plate 3.)

Wings; the side petals of a butterfly-shaped blossom. (Plate 17.)

Winged; applied to seeds: — furnished with a thin, flat membrane on each side: as in the maple.

WOODY; like wood, not herbaceous: as the principal stem of the wall-flower. (Plate 14.)

THE END.

Printed by A. Strahan,
New-Street-Square, London.

CPSIA information can be obtained
at www.ICGtesting.com
Printed in the USA
LVHW081428130720
660536LV00007B/56

9 781354 56118